THE

AS SEEN ON TV

COOKBOOK

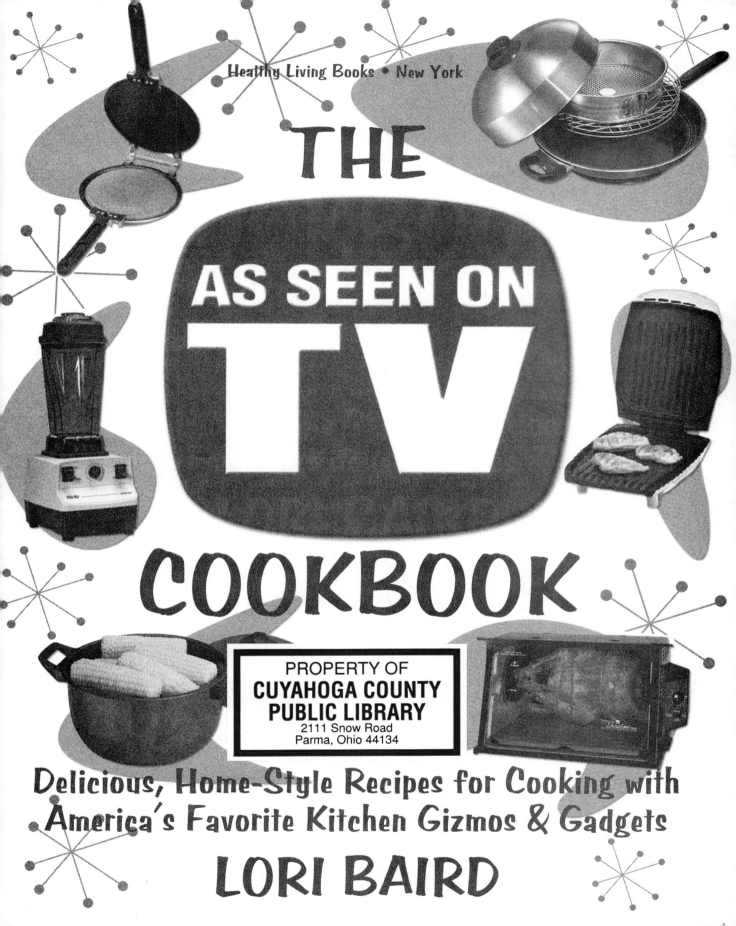

Healthy Living Books • New York

THE

AS SEEN ON TV

COOKBOOK

Delicious, Home-Style Recipes for Cooking with America's Favorite Kitchen Gizmos & Gadgets

LORI BAIRD

Healthy Living Books
Hatherleigh Press
5-22 46th Avenue
Long Island City, NY 11101
1-800-528-2550

Library of Congress Cataloging-in-Publication Data
available upon request.

All Hatherleigh Press titles are available for special
promotions and premiums. For more information,
please contact the manager of our Special Sales
department at 800-528-2550.

Project Credits
Healthy Living Books Staff
President & CEO: Andrew Flach
Publisher: Kevin Moran
Editorial Director: Lori Baird
Art Director & Production Manager: **Tai Blanche**
Manager, Public Relations & Corporate
Communications: Meredith Cosgrove
Associate Editor: Myrsini Stephanides
Designer: Barbara Balch, Tai Blanche
Page Composition: Regina Starace

Printed in Canada on acid-free paper
10 9 8 7 6 5 4 3 2 1

To my husband Tom, who eats everything I cook.

—LB

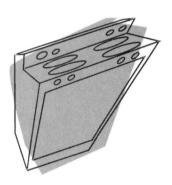

Contents

A Brief History of the Kitchen Gadgets We Love

Look around your kitchen; how many cooking gadgets do you own? If you've picked up this book, chances are your drawers are full to bursting with choppers, corers, slicers, peelers, poachers, blenders, and knives—maybe you've even purchased some of them after watching an infomercial or two.

There's something so American about those ingenious inventions. Each purchase, no matter how financially insignificant, brings with it the promise of saved time and labor—not to mention the undying adoration of family and friends who will think you slaved for hours! Sometimes these gadgets simply make preparing food more fun. Sure, you *could* whip up a batch of flapjacks in your old skillet, but wouldn't you rather flip them in your new Perfect Pancake?

The always crafty—sometimes kooky—minds who dream up these amazing gizmos have changed the face of the modern kitchen. And with so many new tools around—from Ginsu Knives and Turbo Cookers to Vita-Mix Blenders and Lean, Mean Grilling Machines—you might think that we're living through the renaissance of kitchen inventions.

2 million years ago
Sticks and sharpened stones are the very latest kitchen tools.

3000 B.C.
Spoons and knives come into vogue, but only for serving food, not for eating it.

400 B.C.
Earliest known eating forks appear in Byzantium. Before then, people ate out of communal pots with their fingers.

ca. 1450
Hooks, pulleys, and chains allow cooks to adjust the distance between the cooking fire and the cooking pot, thus allowing for temperature regulation.

1700
Common folk begin to use plates, which they tote around with them from place to place. Most plates are made of wood, but some—usually owned by the wealthy—are made of metal.

mid-1700s
Europeans begin using forks for eating.

1795
The corkscrew is patented. Before its invention, people pulled corks out of bottles using a tool designed to remove bullets from rifle barrels.

As Seen on TV Fun Fact

29 percent of Americans have purchased products sold on TV.

But the history of kitchen gadgetry goes back much further; men and women have been inventing amazing kitchen devices since before recorded history. Think about it: Every single item in your kitchen—from the microwave and refrigerator to the butter knife and soup spoon—was once *the* latest thing, the innovation that promised to revolutionize the way people prepared and served food. In fact, some of the items we take most for granted were once considered so bizarre that they didn't catch on for centuries. (Keep that in mind the next time someone makes fun of your Inside the Shell Egg Scrambler.)

Here's a look at some of the pioneer inventions that paved the way for our favorite modern kitchen tools.

The Early Days

The prehistoric kitchen was equipped with little more than a modest selection of pointy sticks and rocks. These hardly seem like breakthrough devices by modern standards, but using (or creating) tools to simplify common tasks is the innovation at the heart of all kitchen gadgetry. Though these earliest tools neither sliced or diced, they did make the tasks of poking, prodding, cracking and grinding easier for the early kitchen dweller. With the discovery of fire half a million years later, the capabilities of the ancestral kitchen grew by leaps and bounds. Instead of slaving over a cold carcass, man could now whip up a hot meal. Several millennia later, in the Middle Ages, the art of igniting the flame was mastered. The new challenge of the day was temperature regulation—setting the old cauldron right in

the fire wasn't exactly precision cooking. That lead to the next amazing breakthrough: the idea of using hooks and pulleys to adjust the position of the cauldron relative to the fire.

Imagine living back then and suddenly having the ability to enjoy a meal that was neither stone cold nor searingly hot. Could it possibly get any better?

Well, yes, because Europeans at least were still eating out of a common pot with their fingers. Spoons and carving knives were common—but for some reason weren't used for anything except *serving* food. Imagine the muss and the fuss—and the laundry bills.

Eating forks were common in Byzantium at the time, but when an industrious Brit brought one home to show his friends, he was ridiculed—the British considered forks effeminate. Why would a person use a fork when God gave him two perfectly good hands? And the English weren't the only ones: The French considered fork use a silly affectation. It wasn't until the 18th century that Europeans conceded that forks weren't such a bad idea.

1803
Apple parer is invented.

1810
The can (aka tin canister) is invented by Peter Durand, whose goal is to supply the British Navy with provisions. (Note that the can opener isn't invented until 1858. Before then cans were ripped open with knives, bayonets, and even rife fire.)

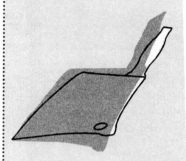

1850
Cook stoves come into widespread use, closing the chapter of the dangerous, dirty, open hearth, and the back-breaking work of lifting and moving heavy iron cookware.

1858
First can opener is invented, in Waterbury, Connecticut. The dangerous contraption is replaced by a safer design in 1870.

During the 19th century:

- More than 185 patents were issued for coffee grinders
- More than 500 patents were issued for apple/ potato peelers

1858 (con't)
The Mason Jar is invented by John Mason.

1869
Waffle iron patented.

1884
Egg beater patented.

1885
Electric mixer invented.

1886
The word *gadget* first appears in the English language.

The first practical dishwasher is invented by wealthy Shelbyville, Illinois, hostess, Josephine Cochraine. It was used mostly by hotels and restaurants.

ca. 1890
Electric stove introduced.

1893
First electric toaster invented in England.

1892
The thermos is invented. Hot soup for lunch!

As Seen on TV Fun Fact

The Veg-O-Matic II is enshrined in the permanent collection of the Smithsonian National Museum of American History.

The Industrial Revolution

Time marched on and so did the parade of new time-, labor-, and money-saving contraptions. Perhaps the one invention that most affected everyday life was the cookstove, which came about in 1850. Before then, the hearth was the center of the family home, and although it sounds heart-warming, bending and lifting, moving heavy pots and pans, and keeping the fire going day and night were non-stop, back-breaking jobs. The new-fangled cookstove allowed women to cook at waist level (so long aching back) and regulate cooking temperature (goodbye burnt bread). The downside? The stove replaced the hearth, which had been the traditional family gathering place, and so was blamed by some for the decline of family life.

After the invention of the cookstove, things really took off; the industrial revolution brought with it an explosion of ideas: Before 1860, the United States government had issued a grand total of 36,000 patents. In just thirty years, between 1860 and 1890, an additional *400,000* novel ideas were patented. Among them were such marvels as the drinking straw, egg beater, electric mixer, electric stove, milkshake maker, and waffle iron. In fact, the word *gadget* was coined in 1886 to mean any small handy kitchen tool.

The Modern Era

Fast forward to the mid-twentieth century, to the crossroads that forever changed the face of kitchen gadgetry: The introduction of television to the American public in 1946 and the broadcast of the very first infomercial in 1950. (Actually, the word infomercial—a combination of the words information and commercial—wasn't coined until 1981.)

The product? It wasn't the Veg-O-Matic; the Ronco invention came along a few years later. The very first kitchen gadget pitched on television was the Vita-Mix blender. In that 30-minute spot, Vita-Mix founder W.G. "Papa" Barnard demonstrated his new blender on WEWS-TV for thousands of viewers. The only hitch was that Barnard didn't have "operators standing by," and so he spent the night sitting on his bed taking orders over the phone.

A flurry of inventions and infomercials followed. Leading the charge was Ron Popiel—crown prince of infomercial pitchmen—first with the Chop-O-Matic ("You'll chop onions so fine. . . without shedding a single tear.") and then the Veg-O-Matic ("Simply turn the dial, and change from thin to thick slices.") in the early sixties.

1896
Lemon squeezer is patented by American John Thomas White.

1916
Frigidaire invents the first electric refrigerator.

1922
First blender is invented, paving the way for frozen margaritas and smoothies.

1926
Pop-up toaster invented.

1927
First garbage disposal invented.

Cheese slicer is invented by Norwegian Thor Bjorkland.

1938
Teflon is invented.

1946
Television first introduced to the public.

Tupperware hits the market and Tupperware parties become the rage throughout the 1950s.

As Seen on TV Fun Facts

- Infomercials air 10,000 times each day.
- Infomercial viewers buy more than $115 billion worth of products each year.
- Women over the age of 40 comprise 80 percent of infomercial consumers.

Source: Washington Post Home Edition, Section E Page 29, November 17, 2002.

1947
Reynold's Wrap aluminum foil is sold for the first time.

1949
The start of the television boom. In 1949, 940,000 households owned a television set. That number grows to 20 million by 1953.

The first infomercial—for the Vita-Mix blender—debuts in Cleveland, Ohio.

1950s
Dishwashers for the home come into use and the term "dishpan hands" begins to disappear from the lexicon.

1952
Tappan introduces the first home microwave oven, which costs a whopping $1,295.

1955
More than 80 percent of American households own a refrigerator.

1956
A 21-year-old named Ron Popeil produces an infomercial for the Chop-O-Matic, paving the way for thousands of infomercials to come.

1975
Ginsu Knives make their debut.

1984
FCC frees local television stations to air longer commercials and the airwaves are flooded with infomercials.

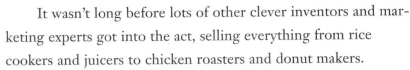

It wasn't long before lots of other clever inventors and marketing experts got into the act, selling everything from rice cookers and juicers to chicken roasters and donut makers.

And *that* brings us back to the *As Seen on TV Cookbook*. In these pages are nearly 150 recipes for some of the very best kitchen inventions sold on television. Among the gadgets we feature are Ronco's Showtime Rotisserie Oven, George Foreman's Lean, Mean Fat Reducing Grilling Machine and Contact Roaster, and even Vita-Mix, which is still making blenders today!

But wait—there's more! We even provide you with all the information you need to order the products in the book. So preheat the Perfect Pancake, turn on the Turbo Cooker, and rev up the Ronco Rotisserie Oven—it's time to start cooking!

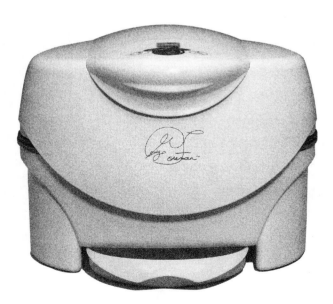

Recipe Quick Reference Guide

Breakfast Entrées

Lunch & Dinner Entrées

Beef

Lamb & Pork

Poultry

Seafood

Pasta

Side Dishes

Beverages

Snacks & Sandwiches

Desserts

Donut Express

Ever since some clever baker in sixteenth-century Holland twisted some scraps of dough into a decorative knot, deep fried it, and dipped it in powdered sugar, the donut has been a staple of many a morning routine.

The problem with donuts is two-fold. First of all, making them at home is a messy endeavor. You need about six cups of cooking oil, which inevitably ends up splattering all over the stove. Second of all, deep-fried donuts are loaded with fat. In fact, the Dutch called them *olykoeks*, or "oily cakes."

Okay, so maybe there's no such thing as a "healthy" donut, but the Donut Express goes a long way toward making the at-home process a lot easier and the product a lot less fatty. To use the Donut Express, you simply prepare the batter as directed, pour it into the pan, and pop it in the oven. No deep-frying, no mess. Sound simple? It certainly is. In fact, after using the Donut Express you may never eat another store-bought donut again. You may even find yourself baking oven fresh donuts for the neighborhood.

Snacks & Sandwiches

MAKES 1 DOZEN
Prep Time: **10 minutes**
Baking Time: **10 minutes**

Chocolate Donuts

2 cups all-purpose flour
⅓ cup unsweetened cocoa powder
2 tablespoons baking powder
½ teaspoon salt
1 cup granulated sugar
½ cup brown sugar
1 ⅓ cups milk
2 eggs
1 tablespoon vegetable shortening

1. Preheat oven to 400°F. Grease donut cups with butter or vegetable oil.

2. In a large bowl, sift together the flour, cocoa, baking powder, and salt. Add the sugars, milk, eggs, and shortening. Stir with a spatula until well combined.

3. Fill the donut cups half full. Bake 10 minutes. Transfer baking pan to a wire rack and cool completely before removing donuts. Glaze or fill cooled donuts as desired.

Nutrition Facts Per Serving: 220 cal.; 5g protein; 3g fat; 45g carb.; 1g fiber; 39mg chol.; 369g sodium

Dandy Donut Tip

Allow the donuts to cool before you remove them from the tray.

Lemon Donuts

Snacks & Sandwiches

MAKES 1 DOZEN
Prep Time: **10 minutes**
Baking Time: **10 minutes**

2 cups all-purpose flour
2 tablespoons baking powder
½ teaspoon salt
½ cup granulated sugar
2 eggs
1 tablespoon lemon extract
1 cup milk
1 tablespoon vegetable shortening

1. Preheat oven to 400°F. Grease donut cups with butter or vegetable oil.

2. In a large bowl, sift together the flour, baking powder, and salt. Add the sugar, eggs, lemon extract, milk, and shortening. Stir with a spatula until well combined.

3. Fill the donut cups half full. Bake 10 minutes. Transfer baking pan to a wire rack and cool completely before removing donuts. Glaze or fill cooled donuts as desired.

Nutrition Facts Per Serving: 147 cal.; 4g protein; 3g fat; 26g carb.; <1g fiber; 38mg chol.; 362g sodium

Spiced Donuts

For the donuts

2 cups all-purpose flour
2 tablespoons baking powder
½ teaspoon salt
2 teaspoons cinnamon
½ teaspoon nutmeg
½ cup granulated sugar
½ cup brown sugar
1 cup milk
2 eggs
1 tablespoon vegetable shortening

For the cinnamon & sugar coating

½ cup sugar
½ cup powdered sugar
1 tablespoon cinnamon

1. Preheat oven to 400°F. Grease donut cups with butter or vegetable oil.

2. For the donuts, in a large bowl, sift together the flour, baking powder, and salt. Add 2 teaspoons cinnamon, the nutmeg, sugars, milk, eggs, and shortening. Stir with a spatula until well combined.

3. Fill the donut cups half full. Bake 10 minutes. Transfer baking pan to a wire rack and cool completely before removing donuts.

4. Meanwhile, to prepare the cinnamon and sugar coating, in a medium bowl, combine the sugar, powdered sugar, and cinnamon. Roll cooled donuts in mixture.

Nutrition Facts Per Serving: 233 cal.; 4g protein; 3g fat; 49g carb.; 1g fiber; 38mg chol.; 365g sodium

Donuts became popular in the United States after the Salvation Army fed them to troops during World War I. Those donuts were cooked in garbage pails and served on bayonets.

Vanilla Donuts

Snacks & Sandwiches

MAKES 1 DOZEN
Prep Time: **10 minutes**
Baking Time: **10 minutes**

2 cups all-purpose flour
2 tablespoons baking powder
½ teaspoon salt
1 cup granulated sugar
1 cup milk
2 eggs
1 teaspoon vanilla
1 tablespoon vegetable shortening

1. Preheat oven to 400°F. Grease donut cups with butter or vegetable oil.

2. In a large bowl, sift together the flour, baking powder, and salt. Add the sugar, milk, eggs, vanilla, and shortening. Stir with a spatula until well combined.

3. Fill the donut cups half full. Bake 10 minutes. Transfer baking pan to a wire rack and cool completely before removing donuts. Glaze or fill the donuts as desired.

Nutrition Facts Per Serving: 176 cal.; 4g protein; 3g fat; 34g carb.; <1g fiber; 38mg chol.; 362g sodium

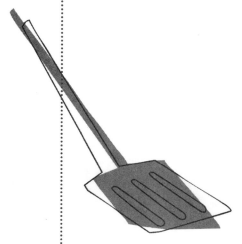

Old-Fashioned Donut Glazes & Icings

For the Old-Fashioned Glaze
2 cups powdered sugar
2 tablespoons corn syrup
sprinkles or jimmies

For the Chocolate Glaze
¼ cup unsweetened cocoa powder
2 cups powdered sugar
2 tablespoons corn syrup

For the Strawberry Icing
½ cup strawberry jelly
2 cups powdered sugar

1. For the Old-Fashioned Glaze, whisk together the powdered sugar and corn syrup. Add water, 1 tablespoon at a time (up to 3 tablespoons) until mixture is thin enough to dip cooled donuts. Top with jimmies or sprinkles, if desired.

2. For the Chocolate Glaze, in a bowl, whisk together the cocoa powder, powdered sugar, and corn syrup. Add water, 1 tablespoon at a time (up to 3 tablespoons) until mixture is thin enough to dip cooled donuts. Top with jimmies or sprinkles, if desired.

3. For the Strawberry Icing, in a bowl, combine the jelly and the powdered sugar. Add water, 1 tablespoon at a time (up to 3 tablespoons) until mixture is thin enough to spread on cooled donuts. Top with jimmies or sprinkles, if desired.

Nutrition Facts Per Serving

Old-Fashioned Glaze: 87 cal.; <1g protein; <1g fat; 23g carb.; <1g fiber; <1mg chol.; 4g sodium

Chocolate Glaze: 92 cal.; <1g protein; <1g fat; 23g carb.; <1g fiber; <1mg chol.; 5g sodium

Strawberry Icing: 111 cal.; <1g protein; <1g fat; 23g carb.; <1g fiber; <1mg chol.; <1g sodium

Donut Shoppe Fillings

Snacks & Sandwiches

EACH FLAVOR MAKES
ENOUGH TO FILL
1 DOZEN DONUTS

Prep Time: **5 minutes**
Cooking Time: **None**

For Jelly Filling
1 ¼ cup strawberry (or other flavor) jelly
¼ cup corn syrup

For Custard Filling
14 ounces sweetened condensed milk
8 ounces instant vanilla pudding

For Chocolate Filling
4 tablespoons solid vegetable shortening
2 cups powdered sugar
¼ cup unsweetened cocoa powder

1. To make the Jelly Filling, in a medium bowl, combine the jelly and corn syrup until well blended.

2. To make the Custard Filling, in a medium bowl, combine the condensed milk and instant pudding until well blended.

3. To make the Chocolate Filling, in a medium bowl, beat the vegetable shortening with an electric mixer until light and fluffy. Beat in powdered sugar, 1 cup at a time, until mixture is creamy. Add the cocoa powder and ¼ cup cold water and continue to beat until mixture is fluffy.

4. To fill cooled donuts, scoop one filling flavor into the Donut Express Pastry Injector. Insert the tip of the injector into a donut. Release the filling by pressing the injector handle to no more than 1 bevel.

Nutrition Facts Per Serving

Jelly Filling: 102 cal.; <1g protein; <1g fat; 27g carb.; <1g fiber; <1mg chol.; 8g sodium

Custard Filling: 67 cal.; 3g protein; 3g fat; 33g carb.; <1g fiber; 11mg chol.; 280g sodium

Chocolate Filling: 119 cal.; <1g protein; 4g fat; 21g carb.; <1g fiber; <1mg chol.; <1g sodium

George Foreman
Lean Mean Contact Roasting Machine & Lean Mean Fat Reducing Grilling Machine

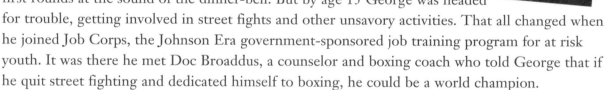

Puncher, preacher, family man, rancher, and pitchman for his own line of products, George Foreman has done it all.

On January 10, 1949, the future two-time world heavyweight champ was born in Marshall, Texas. One of seven children, "Big George" went his first rounds at the sound of the dinner-bell. But by age 15 George was headed for trouble, getting involved in street fights and other unsavory activities. That all changed when he joined Job Corps, the Johnson Era government-sponsored job training program for at risk youth. It was there he met Doc Broaddus, a counselor and boxing coach who told George that if he quit street fighting and dedicated himself to boxing, he could be a world champion.

He was right: George went on to win a gold medal for the United States at the 1968 Mexico City Olympics. He knocked out Joe Frazier in 1973 to win his first world heavyweight championship, and against the odds, at age 45, Foreman knocked out Michael Moorer in the eighth round to become the oldest heavyweight champ.

But wait, there's more: George Foreman is an ordained minister. He started his ministry in 1977; and in 1984 he opened The George Foreman Youth & Community Center.

Even with such a hectic schedule, George found time to become the pitchman for the George Foreman Lean Mean Fat Reducing Grilling Machine and later, the Lean Mean Contact Roasting Machine. The products have been huge hits: The grill has sold more than 40,000,000 units since 1995.

Note: All Contact Roaster recipes are given for the 12-quart Roaster. Directions for the 4-quart roaster are provided in accompanying sidebars.

31

Lunch & Dinner Entrées

SERVES 6
Prep Time: *15 minutes*
Cooking Time: *1 hour, 15 minutes*

Chinese Five-Spice Chicken

1 chicken (4 to 5 pounds), cleaned, giblets removed
2 cloves garlic, minced
2 thin slices fresh ginger
2 tablespoons sesame oil
1 tablespoon Chinese five-spice powder

1. Preheat the 12-quart Contact Roaster. Rub the garlic over the chicken; discard garlic. Rub the ginger slices over chicken; discard ginger. Lightly brush sesame oil over chicken. Dust chicken with five-spice powder.

2. Using oven mitts and a plastic or wooden utensil, place the chicken in the Contact Roaster. Cover and set the Timer for 60 to 75 minutes. The chicken will be done when a meat thermometer inserted into the thickest part of the meat registers at least 180°F. Allow the chicken to stand for 10 minutes before carving. Remove the skin before eating.

Nutrition Facts Per Serving: 459 cal.; 74g protein; 16g fat; 2g carb.; 236mg chol.; 274g sodium

To prepare the chicken in the 4-quart roaster, select a 3- to 4-pound chicken and roast for 60 minutes as directed above. Serves 3 to 4.

Flank Steak Rolled with Gorgonzola, Walnuts & Parsley

Lunch & Dinner Entrées

SERVES 8
Prep Time: 15 minutes
Cooking Time: 1 hour, 20 minutes

For the stuffing

1 ½ cups soft bread crumbs
1 cup gorgonzola cheese, crumbled
½ cup walnuts, finely chopped
¼ cup white onions, minced
¼ cup fresh parsley, chopped
1 teaspoon garlic, minced

For the steak

1 to 2 pounds flank steak
1 cup prepared steak marinade

1. For the stuffing, mix together the bread crumbs, cheese, walnuts, onions, parsley, and garlic. Place the steak on a flat work surface and discard the marinade. Shape the stuffing mixture down the middle third of the steak lengthwise and fold the 2 sides over the middle. Use cooking string to tie the rolled steak as tightly as possible.

2. Preheat the 12-quart Contact Roaster: Using oven mitts and a wooden or plastic spatula, place the flank steak on the Wire Rack in the Contact Roaster. Set the Timer for 70 to 80 minutes. An internal meat thermometer will register 145°F for rare. Cook longer if desired. Remove the steak from the Contact Roaster and let stand for 10 minutes. Slice in 1-inch thick pieces.

Nutrition Facts Per Serving: 311 cal.; 15g protein; 5g fat; 26g carb.; 45mg chol.; 747g sodium

To prepare the steak in the 4-quart roaster, cook for 60 to 70 minutes as directed above and test for doneness. Cook longer according to your preference.

Lunch & Dinner Entrées

SERVES 12

Prep Time: **15 minutes**

Cooking Time: **2 hours, 40 minutes**

Greek Roasted Lamb with Rosemary Potatoes

3 tablespoons extra virgin olive oil

5 large Russet potatoes, scrubbed, unpeeled and roughly cut into eighths

1 teaspoon salt

1 teaspoon freshly ground black pepper

2 tablespoons extra virgin olive oil

1 bone-in leg of lamb (5 to 6 pounds), visible fat removed

¼ cup fresh rosemary, finely minced, divided

5 cloves garlic, minced

1 teaspoon ground black pepper

1. Preheat the 12-quart Contact Roaster. In a large bowl, combine the oil, potatoes, salt, and pepper. Set aside. Using oven mitts and a plastic or wooden utensil, place the leg of lamb on the inverted Wire Rack in the Contact Roaster. Drizzle lamb with the olive oil; sprinkle with half of the rosemary, garlic, and pepper. Set the Timer for 60 minutes.

2. Carefully open the Contact Roaster and add the potatoes around the lamb. Sprinkle with the remaining rosemary. Reset the Timer for 70 to 100 minutes. Test the lamb for doneness by inserting a meat thermometer into the thickest part of the meat. The thermometer should register at least 150°F for rare. When done, remove the lamb and potatoes from the Contact Roaster. Let lamb stand 10 minutes before carving. Serve with the roasted potatoes.

Nutrition Facts Per Serving: 470 cal.; 29g protein; 36g fat; 7g carb.; 107mg chol.; 249g sodium

To prepare the lamb in the 4-quart Roaster, select a 3- to 4-pound leg of lamb and decrease the remaining ingredients by one-third. Roast for 70 to 80 minutes and test for doneness as directed above.

Hawaiian Mahi-Mahi with Mango-Pineapple Salsa

Lunch & Dinner Entrées

SERVES 8
Prep Time: **15 minutes**
Cooking Time: **30 minutes**

3 pounds fresh mahi-mahi fillets
salt and white pepper, to taste
2 cups fresh mangoes, diced
2 cups fresh pineapple, diced
½ cup purple onion, minced
½ teaspoon freshly ground black pepper
1 teaspoon salt
2 tablespoons fresh lime juice
fresh cilantro, for garnish

1. Preheat the 12-quart Contact Roaster. Place the fresh fillets in the Baking Pan; add salt and pepper to taste. Using oven mitts, place the Baking Pan in the Contact Roaster and set the Timer for 20 to 30 minutes, or until the fish flakes easily with a fork and is opaque throughout.

2. Prepare the salsa by combining the mangoes, pineapple, onion, black pepper, salt, and lime juice in a large serving bowl. Toss well and refrigerate. When the fish fillets are done, top each with a spoonful of salsa. Garnish each serving with cilantro.

Nutrition Facts Per Serving: 197 cal.; 32g protein; 1g fat; 13g carb.; 125mg chol.; 462g sodium

To prepare the mahi-mahi in the 4-quart Roaster, select 1 to 1½ pounds of mahi-mahi and decrease the remaining ingredients by half. Cook for 20 to 25 minutes as directed above. Serves 3 to 4.

Lunch & Dinner Entrées

SERVES 15
Prep Time: *15 minutes*
Cooking Time: *2 hours, 40 minutes*

Homestyle Roasted Turkey

1 turkey (10 to 12 pounds), cleaned and dried
2 teaspoons salt
2 teaspoons black pepper
2 tablespoons extra virgin olive oil
3 lemons, cut into quarters
1 lime, cut into quarters
2 white onions, peeled and cut into quarters

1. Mix together the salt, pepper, and oil and cover the entire turkey with the spice mixture. Preheat the Contact Roaster.

2. Using oven mitts and a plastic or wooden utensil, place the turkey on the inverted Wire Rack in the 12-quart Contact Roaster. Set the Timer for 130 to 160 minutes. The turkey will be done when the meat thermometer inserted into the thickest part of the meat registers at least 180°F. Let turkey stand for 20 minutes before carving. Remove the skin before serving.

Nutrition Facts Per Serving: 485 cal.; 83g protein; 13g fat; 4g carb.; 246mg chol.; 653g sodium

Hot Sauced Bayou Shrimp

4 pounds uncooked large shrimp, peeled and deveined, tails removed
3 cloves garlic, minced
juice of 2 lemons
¼ cup vegetable oil
1 tablespoon bottled hot sauce
1 ½ teaspoons chili powder
1 tablespoon tomato paste
1 teaspoon salt

1. Place the shrimp in a large, sealable plastic bag. Whisk together the garlic, lemon juice, oil, hot sauce, chili powder, tomato paste, and salt and pour over the shrimp. Mix the shrimp with the sauce, coating each piece thoroughly and refrigerate for 1 hour.

2. Preheat the 12-quart Contact Roaster. Place the shrimp in the Baking Pan and discard the sauce. Using oven mitts, place the Baking Pan in the Contact Roaster and set the Timer for 20 to 35 minutes. The shrimp will be done when they are completely pink and opaque throughout. Serve while hot.

Nutrition Facts Per Serving: 124 cal.; 19g protein; 4g fat; 2g carb.; 137mg chol.; 257g sodium

To prepare the shrimp in the 4-quart Contact Roaster, use 2 pounds of shrimp and decrease the recipe ingredients by half. Roast as directed. Serves 10.

Jalapeño Chili Mustard Pork Tenderloin

2 pounds pork tenderloin
2 cups grainy Dijon mustard
2 jalapeño chilis, seeded and minced

1. Place the pork tenderloin on the inverted Wire Rack in the 12-quart Contact Roaster. Spoon the Dijon mustard over the top of the pork and sprinkle with the chilies. Set the Timer for 60 to 75 minutes.

2. An internal meat thermometer will register 160°F to 170°F for a medium tenderloin. Cook longer according to your preference, if desired. Remove the pork from the Contact Roaster and let stand for 10 minutes. Slice evenly into ½-inch thick pieces.

Nutrition Facts Per Serving: 227 cal.; 23g protein; 6g fat; <1g carb.; 75mg chol.; 1567g sodium

To prepare the tenderloin in the 4-quart Roaster, select a 1- to 1½-pound tenderloin. Decrease the mustard to 1 cup and use only 1 chili. Cook for 45 to 60 minutes and test for doneness as directed above.

Lemon Thyme Roasted Chicken

Lunch & Dinner Entrées

SERVES 5
Prep Time: **15 minutes**
Cooking Time: **1 hour, 15 minutes**

1 chicken (3 to 4 pounds), cleaned, giblets removed
2 tablespoons extra virgin olive oil
1 teaspoon salt
1 teaspoon black pepper
juice of 1 lemon
1 tablespoon fresh thyme, minced
1 tablespoon fresh tarragon, minced
1 tablespoon fresh parsley, minced

1. Preheat the 12-quart Contact Roaster. Brush the oil evenly over the chicken. Sprinkle the salt and pepper over the oil.

2. Using oven mitts and a plastic or wooden utensil, place the chicken in the Contact Roaster and sprinkle with the lemon juice. Lightly cover with the herbs. Cover and set the Timer for 60 to 75 minutes. The chicken will be done when a meat thermometer inserted into the thickest part of the meat registers 180°F. Allow the chicken to stand for 10 minutes before carving. Remove the skin before eating.

Nutrition Facts Per Serving: 462 cal.; 74g protein; 15g fat; 2g carb.; 236mg chol.; 738g sodium

To prepare the chicken in the 4-quart roaster, select a 3- to 4-pound chicken and roast for 60 minutes as directed above. Serves 3 to 4.

Moroccan Salmon Steaks

2 pounds salmon steaks, about 1-inch thick
¼ cup extra virgin olive oil
¼ cup fresh lemon juice
¼ cup fresh parsley, minced
¼ cup fresh cilantro, minced
1 tablespoon fresh gingerroot, grated
1 teaspoon ground cumin
1 clove garlic, minced
1 teaspoon paprika
½ teaspoon salt
¼ teaspoon cayenne pepper
¼ teaspoon black pepper

1. Place the salmon steaks in a shallow glass pan. In a blender, combine the olive oil, lemon juice, parsley, cilantro, gingerroot, cumin, garlic, paprika, salt, cayenne, black pepper, and ¼ cup water. Process on HIGH speed until very smooth. Pour the marinade over the salmon and turn once to coat the steaks. Cover tightly with plastic wrap and refrigerate the steaks for 1 to 4 hours.

2. Preheat the 12-quart Contact Roaster. Place the steaks in the Baking Pan and discard the marinade. Using oven mitts, place the Baking Pan in the Contact Roaster. Set the Timer for 30 minutes. The fish will be done when it flakes easily with a fork. Continue roasting for 10 minutes, if needed.

Nutrition Facts Per Serving: 367 cal.; 367g protein; 25g fat; 2g carb.; 100mg chol.; 268g sodium

To prepare the salmon in the 4-quart Roaster, select 1 pound of salmon steaks and decrease the remaining ingredients by half. Roast for 20 to 30 minutes, or until the fish flakes easily with a fork.

San Antonio Beef Tenderloin

1 cup yellow onion, chopped
1 teaspoon black pepper
1 cup celery, chopped
1 cup red bell pepper, chopped
½ cup green bell pepper, chopped
2 cloves garlic, minced
1 teaspoon dry mustard
1 teaspoon ground cumin
2 tablespoons extra virgin olive oil
½ teaspoon cayenne pepper
½ teaspoon salt
1 teaspoon black pepper
2 to 3 pounds beef tenderloin

1. Invert the Wire Rack and place it in the Contact Roaster: Preheat the 12-quart or the 4-quart Contact Roaster. In a small bowl, mix together all of the ingredients except the beef tenderloin. Make ½-inch-deep cuts over the entire tenderloin and pat the vegetables and seasonings over the tenderloin to form a crust, pressing lightly.

2. Using oven mitts and a plastic or wooden utensil, place the roast on the Wire Rack in the Contact Roaster. Set the Timer for 60 to 90 minutes. An internal meat thermometer should read at least 145°F for rare. Remove the beef from the Contact Roaster; let stand 15 minutes prior to serving. Carve in 1-inch slices and serve immediately.

Nutrition Facts Per Serving: 364 cal.; 21g protein; 29g fat; 5g carb.; 79mg chol.; 216g sodium

Tandoori Turkey Medallions

2 to 3 pounds turkey tenderloins, cut into 12 to 14 pieces
2 cups plain nonfat yogurt
2 tablespoons fresh gingerroot, finely grated
1 clove garlic, minced
2 tablespoons vegetable oil
1 tablespoon ground paprika
2 teaspoons ground cumin
2 teaspoons ground turmeric
¼ teaspoon cayenne pepper
1 teaspoon salt
½ teaspoon black pepper

1. Place the tenderloins in a shallow glass dish. In a medium plastic or glass bowl, combine the yogurt, gingerroot, garlic, vegetable oil, paprika, cumin, turmeric, cayenne, salt, and black pepper. Whisk together and pour over the turkey tenderloins. Cover the turkey with plastic wrap and refrigerate for 4 hours, turning the turkey every hour.

2. Preheat the 12-quart Contact Roaster. Place the turkey in the Baking Pan and discard the marinade. Using oven mitts, place the Baking Pan in the Contact Roaster; set the Timer for 50 to 70 minutes. The turkey medallions will be done when no pink remains and the turkey is hot throughout. Remove and serve while hot.

Nutrition Facts Per Serving: 191 cal.; 31g protein; 4g fat; 6g carb.; 77mg chol.; 389g sodium

To prepare the turkey in the 4-quart Roaster, select 1 to 2 pounds of turkey tenderloin and decrease the remaining ingredients by half. Roast the turkey for 30 to 40 minutes as directed above. Serves 3 to 4.

Baby Spinach Salad with Asparagus & Sesame Cilantro Dressing

Side Dishes

SERVES 6
Prep Time: **15 minutes**
Cooking Time: **35 minutes**

*3 pounds fresh tender asparagus, trimmed to no more than
    6 inches long*
6 cups baby spinach leaves, cleaned and crisped in the refrigerator
*1 cup romaine lettuce leaves, washed, torn and crisped in the
    refrigerator*
2 large tomatoes, seeded and diced
3 tablespoons sweet onion, minced
3 cloves garlic, minced
2 tablespoons fresh cilantro, chopped
2 teaspoons sesame oil
salt and pepper, to taste

1. Do not preheat the Contact Roaster. Pour 2 cups water into the Baking Pan and place in the 12-quart Contact Roaster. Place the Wire Rack in the Baking Pan and arrange the asparagus on the rack, layering as evenly as possible. Cover and set the Timer for 25 to 35 minutes. Check the asparagus when the Timer goes off. The asparagus will be tender-crisp when done. Remove from the Wire Rack and cool slightly.

2. For the salad, toss together the spinach, lettuce, tomatoes, onion, garlic, and cilantro. Portion the salad onto 6 individual plates. Cover each serving with the asparagus and drizzle with the sesame oil. Sprinkle with salt and pepper to taste. Serve immediately.

Nutrition Facts Per Serving: 90 cal.; 9g protein; 2g fat; 15g carb.; 0mg chol.; 61g sodium

To prepare the salad in the 4-quart Contact Roaster, decrease the ingredients by half and cook the asparagus in the Baking Pan in ½ cup water for 20 to 25 minutes, or until tender-crisp. Serves 3 to 4.

Side Dishes

SERVES 6
Prep Time: **15 minutes**
Cooking Time: **45 minutes**

Herb & Bacon-Stuffed Walla Walla Onions

6 Walla Walla onions, peeled
5 cups peasant-style bread, cut into small cubes
½ cup chicken broth
1 tablespoon virgin olive oil
3 cloves garlic, minced
3 slices turkey bacon, cooked and crumbled
⅓ cup Parmesan cheese, grated
2 tablespoons fresh parsley, minced
1 ½ teaspoons salt
1 teaspoon black pepper

1. Preheat the 12-quart Contact Roaster. Cut part of the bottom off each onion so that it will stand in the Baking Pan. Cut across the top of the onion and remove inner core, leaving a ¼-inch wall of onion layers. Dice the inner layers of the onions. In a large bowl, mix together the onions, bread cubes, broth, oil, garlic, bacon, cheese, parsley, salt, and pepper. Toss well to combine.

2. Pack each onion with the herb stuffing and place the onions in the Baking Pan. Using oven mitts, place the Baking Pan in the Contact Roaster and set the Timer for 30 to 45 minutes. The onions will be done when soft to the touch and lightly browned.

Nutrition Facts Per Serving: 230 cal.; 8g protein; 7g fat; 34g carb.; 9mg chol.; 1070g sodium

To prepare the onions in the 4-quart Contact Roaster, substitute 3 to 4 onions and decrease the remaining ingredients by half. Roast the onions for 30 minutes and test for doneness as directed above. Serves 4.

Roasted Yukon Gold Potatoes with Rosemary

Side Dishes

SERVES 6
Prep Time: **10 minutes**
Cooking Time: **1 hour, 10 minutes**

6 Yukon Gold potatoes, cleaned
1 ½ teaspoons salt
1 teaspoon freshly ground black pepper
2 tablespoons virgin olive oil
2 tablespoons rosemary, snipped
1 tablespoon Italian flat-leaf parsley, minced

1. Preheat the 12-quart Contact Roaster. Cut the potatoes into eighths and place in the Baking Pan. Sprinkle with salt and pepper; drizzle with the oil. Cover the potatoes with the rosemary and parsley.

2. Using oven mitts, place the Baking Pan in the Contact Roaster and set Timer for 70 minutes. A fork will easily pass through the flesh of the potatoes when done. Roast for an additional 10 minutes, if needed. Remove the potatoes from the Contact Roaster and serve immediately.

Nutrition Facts Per Serving: 75 cal.; 3g protein; 4g fat; 9g carb.; 12mg chol.; 448g sodium

To prepare the potatoes in the 4-quart Contact Roaster, substitute 4 potatoes, 1 teaspoon salt, ½ teaspoon black pepper, and 1 tablespoon each olive oil and rosemary. Sprinkle with 2 teaspoons Italian parsley. Roast for 60 minutes as directed above. Serves 4.

Roasted Corn & Red Peppers with Blue Tortilla Chips

3 cups fresh corn kernels (you may substitute frozen
   or canned, drained corn)
1 jalapeño pepper, seeded and minced
1 red bell pepper, cored, seeded and chopped
½ cup white onion, chopped
1 tablespoon extra virgin olive oil
1 cup egg substitute
salt and black pepper to taste
¼ cup Parmesan cheese, finely grated
8 ounces baked blue corn tortilla chips

1. Preheat the 12-quart Contact Roaster. Place the corn, peppers, and onion in the Baking Pan and drizzle with the olive oil.

2. Using oven mitts, place the Baking Pan in the Contact Roaster and set the Timer for 10 minutes. Cook, stirring once with a plastic spatula while roasting. Remove the Baking Pan from the Contact Roaster and pour the egg substitute over the vegetables; sprinkle with the salt and pepper to taste. Sprinkle evenly with the cheese and return to the Contact Roaster, setting the Timer for 20 minutes. Remove when the egg substitute is set and serve with tortilla chips.

Nutrition Facts Per Serving: 233 cal.; 9g protein; 5g fat; 38g carb.; 2mg chol.; 580g sodium

To prepare the corn and peppers in the 4-quart Contact Roaster, decrease the ingredients by half. Cook the corn, peppers, and onion for 10 minutes as directed above. Cook the vegetables and egg for a total of 10 minutes as directed above. Serves 4.

Spinach & Green Onion Vegetable Roll-Ups

Snacks & Sandwiches

MAKES 36 PIECES
Prep Time: **20 minutes,** *plus chilling*
Cooking Time: **10 minutes**

10 ounces frozen chopped spinach, thawed and squeezed dry
1 cup canned artichokes, packed in water, drained
½ cup black olives, chopped
¼ cup green onions, thinly sliced
8 ounces nonfat cream cheese, softened
½ cup nonfat mayonnaise
1 teaspoon black pepper
dash bottled hot sauce
4 low-fat flour tortillas (9 inches each)
nonfat cooking spray

1. In a medium bowl, mix together the spinach, artichokes, olives, and onions. Toss to mix well. Add the cream cheese, mayonnaise, pepper, and hot sauce. Blend well.

2. To assemble, place 1 tortilla on a flat work surface. Cover each with one quarter of the spinach spread, leaving a ½-inch margin around the edge. Roll up the tortilla and tightly cover in plastic wrap. Repeat with the remaining roll-ups. Refrigerate for 1 hour.

3. Preheat the 12-quart Contact Roaster. Unwrap the tortillas and cut into 1-inch-thick slices. Place the slices, cut side down, in the Baking Pan and use oven mitts to place the Baking Pan in the Contact Roaster. Cook the roll-ups for 8 to 10 minutes, or until warm and softened.

Nutrition Facts Per Serving: 103 cal.; 3g protein; 1g fat; 17g carb.; 0mg chol.; 543g sodium

To prepare the Roll-Ups in the 4-quart Contact Roaster, place one-half of the roll-ups in the Baking Pan and cook as directed. Repeat with the remaining Roll-Ups.

Desserts

SERVES 10
Prep Time: **15 minutes**
Cooking Time: **50 minutes**

A "Lighter" Chocolate Cake

2 cups all-purpose flour
1 cup sugar
¾ cup unsweetened cocoa
¼ cup plus 2 tablespoons cornstarch
¾ teaspoon baking soda
¾ teaspoons salt
1 ½ teaspoons vanilla extract
¾ cup egg substitute
¾ cup light or dark corn syrup
powdered sugar for dusting
nonfat cooking spray

1. Preheat the 12-quart Contact Roaster. Coat the Baking Pan with the cooking spray. In a large bowl, combine the flour, sugar, cocoa, cornstarch, baking soda, and the salt until thoroughly mixed. In a medium bowl, whisk the vanilla, egg substitute, corn syrup, and 1 ½ cups water to blend. Stir the egg mixture into the dry ingredients until smooth. Pour the batter into the Baking Pan.

2. Using oven mitts, place the Baking Pan into the Contact Roaster. Close the Lid and set the Timer for 45 to 50 minutes. The cake will be done when a toothpick inserted in the center comes out clean. Using oven mitts, remove the Baking Pan from the Contact Roaster and cool on a wire rack. Dust the top of the cake with the powdered sugar.

Nutrition Facts Per Serving: 288 cal.; 6g protein; 1g fat; 68g carb.; 0mg chol.; 332g sodium

To prepare the cake in the 4-quart Contact Roaster, decrease the ingredients by one-third. Bake for 30 to 40 minutes and test the cake for doneness as directed above. Serves 4.

Duo Strawberry Galette

9 ounces frozen puff pastry, thawed
3 cups fresh strawberries, cleaned and hulled
1 tablespoon unsalted butter, cut into small pieces
2 tablespoons sugar
3 tablespoons strawberry jelly
pinch salt

1. Place the thawed puff pastry in the Baking Pan and loosely shape into a circle. Place the strawberries, hull side down, over the pastry in a circular fashion. Cover the pastry leaving a 1-inch border all around. Fold in the edges of the pastry over the top of the strawberries. Dot the strawberries with the butter and sprinkle with the sugar.

2. Preheat the 12-quart Contact Roaster. Using oven mitts, place the Baking Pan in the Contact Roaster and set the Timer for 40 to 50 minutes, or until the fruit is soft. Remove the Galette and cool on a rack for 20 minutes.

3. While the Galette cools, heat the strawberry jelly, salt, and 1 tablespoon water in a small saucepan. Heat and stir until the sauce starts to simmer. Remove from the heat and brush the strawberry Galette with the glaze, covering the strawberries evenly.

Nutrition Facts Per Serving: 237 cal.; 3g protein; 4g fat; 26g carb.; 4mg chol.; 117g sodium

To prepare the Galette in the 4-quart Contact Roaster, decrease all of the ingredients by half and cook for 30 to 40 minutes as directed above. Serves 4.

Farmhouse Raspberry & Apple Crumble

8 tart baking apples, peeled, cored, and thinly sliced
2 cups fresh raspberries (you may substitute frozen, thawed
 raspberries, if desired)
2 tablespoons sugar
1 cup all-purpose flour
⅓ cup sugar
2 teaspoons ground cinnamon
½ cup butter or margarine, softened
½ cup quick-cooking or regular rolled oats
¼ cup walnuts, chopped
nonfat cooking spray

1. Coat the Baking Pan with nonstick cooking spray and preheat the Contact Roaster. Combine the apples and raspberries in a medium mixing bowl and toss with the 2 tablespoons of sugar.

2. In another bowl, combine the flour, remaining sugar and cinnamon. Cut in the butter with a pastry blender or 2 knives until the mixture resembles crumbs and the butter is evenly distributed. Stir in the oats and walnuts.

3. Spoon the apples and raspberries into the Baking Pan. Scatter the crumbled mixture over the fruit, covering it evenly. Using oven mitts, place the Baking Pan in the 12-quart Contact Roaster and set the Timer for 60 to 70 minutes. The crumble is done when the fruit is very soft and tender and heated throughout.

Nutrition Facts Per Serving: 310 cal.; 3g protein; 12g fat; 51g carb.; 25mg chol.; 94g sodium

To prepare the Crumble in the 4-quart Contact Roaster, use 4 baking apples and decrease the remaining ingredients by half. Cook for 40 to 50 minutes as directed above. Serves 5 to 6.

Sweet Toffee Roasted Apples

Desserts

SERVES 8
Prep Time: **15 minutes**
Cooking Time: **45 minutes**

8 tart baking apples, peeled and cored
¼ cup butter or margarine, softened
½ cup hard toffee candies, crushed
2 ounces almonds, chopped
¼ cup powdered sugar

1. Cut a thin slice from the bottom of each apple so that it will stand upright, and then place each in the Baking Pan. In a small bowl, mix together the butter, candies, almonds, and powdered sugar. Pack the center of each apple with the toffee stuffing.

2. Preheat the 12-quart Contact Roaster. Using oven mitts, place the Baking Pan into the Contact Roaster and set the Timer for 35 to 45 minutes. The apples will be ready when they are just tender.

Nutrition Facts Per Serving: 267 cal.; 2g protein; 4g fat; 41g carb.; 20mg chol.; 90g sodium

To prepare the apples in the 4-quart Contact Roaster, use 4 apples and decrease the remaining ingredients by half. Cook for 25 to 35 minutes as directed above. Serves 4.

Lunch & Dinner
Entrées

SERVES 6
Prep Time: **20 minutes**
Cooking Time: **8 minutes**

Bacon & Mushroom Stuffed Pork Chops

4 to 6 pork loin chops, 1-inch thick
salt and black pepper, to taste
4 slices turkey bacon
¼ cup white onion, minced
1 clove garlic, minced
1 cup white button mushrooms, chopped
⅛ teaspoon ground black pepper
2 tablespoons balsamic-flavored olive oil
nonfat cooking spray

1. Remove any excess fat from the pork chops. Using a sharp knife, cut a deep pocket into the center of each chop without cutting all the way through the pork. Salt and pepper the chops to taste. Set aside.

2. Saute the bacon in a skillet until crisp; transfer to a paper towel, and then crumble.

3. Pour off all but 1 teaspoon bacon fat from the skillet. Heat the skillet and add the onion and garlic; saute until the onion is translucent. Add the mushrooms and continue sauteing until the mushrooms are tender.

4. Remove the skillet from the heat and stir in the black pepper and the crumbled bacon. Stuff each pork chop with the mushroom and bacon filling; use a toothpick to close the pocket edges.

5. Lightly brush both sides of the pork chops with the balsamic-flavored oil. Spray the grill with cooking spray and preheat for 5 minutes.

6. Grill the stuffed pork chops for 6 to 8 minutes, or until the pork is completely cooked.

Nutrition Facts Per Serving: 216 cal.; 17g protein; 16g fat; 1g carb.; 57mg chol.; 198g sodium

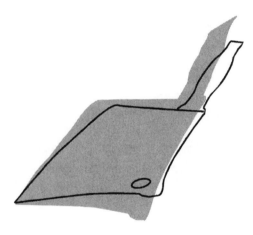

Lunch & Dinner
Entrées

SERVES 4
Prep Time: **10 minutes,
plus marinating**
Cooking Time: **9 minutes**

Coconut-Grilled Swordfish

½ cup low-fat coconut milk
¼ teaspoon ground cinnamon
2 tablespoons light brown sugar
2 tablespoons fresh lemon juice
½ teaspoon salt
4 swordfish steaks, about 6 ounces each
nonfat cooking spray
shredded coconut, for garnish

1. Mix together the coconut milk, cinnamon, brown sugar, lemon juice, and salt. Place the steaks in a shallow glass baking dish and cover with the marinade. Cover tightly and refrigerate 1 to 4 hours.

2. Lightly coat the grill with cooking spray and preheat 5 minutes.

3. Grill the swordfish for 6 to 9 minutes, or until the fish flakes easily and is cooked through completely. Sprinkle steaks with coconut and serve.

Nutrition Facts Per Serving: 261 cal.; 34g protein; 9g fat; 8g carb.; 66mg chol.; 449g sodium

Fiery Sweet Grilled Chicken Breasts

Lunch & Dinner Entrées

SERVES 4
Prep Time: **10 minutes, plus marinating**
Cooking Time: **7 minutes**

4 boneless, skinless chicken breast halves
2 tablespoons low-sodium soy sauce
2 tablespoons hoisin sauce
2 tablespoons chili sauce
¼ cup honey
¼ cup vinegar
3 cloves garlic, minced
½ teaspoon chili powder
½ teaspoon black pepper
nonfat cooking spray

1. Place the chicken breasts in a large glass pan. In a separate bowl, mix together the soy sauce, hoisin sauce, chili sauce, honey, vinegar, garlic, chili powder, and black pepper. Completely cover the chicken with the sauce and refrigerate for 2 to 6 hours.

2. Lightly coat the grill with cooking spray and preheat for 5 minutes.

3. Place the chicken in the grill and cook for 5 to 7 minutes, or until no pink remains.

Nutrition Facts Per Serving: 178 cal.; 17g protein; 1g fat; 25g carb.; 41mg chol.; 719g sodium

Ginger-Grilled Beef & Rice Bowls

Lunch & Dinner Entrées

SERVES 4

Prep Time: **10 minutes, plus marinating**

Cooking Time: **7 minutes**

2 rib eye steaks, about 6 ounces each
1 tablespoon brown sugar
½ tablespoon rice vinegar
2 cloves garlic, finely minced
1 teaspoon ground ginger
1 teaspoon dry mustard powder
1 tablespoon Worcestershire sauce
1 teaspoon fresh lemon juice
2 teaspoons black pepper
nonfat cooking spray
4 cups cooked long-grain white rice

1. Remove any visible fat from the steaks and place the steaks in a flat glass pan. Combine the brown sugar, vinegar, garlic, ginger, mustard power, Worcestershire, lemon juice, and black pepper in a medium bowl and mix well. Pour the marinade over the steaks and chill for at least 1 hour in the refrigerator.

2. Coat the grill with cooking spray and preheat for 5 minutes.

3. Grill the steaks for 5 to 7 minutes, or to desired doneness. To serve, thinly slice the beef and place it on top of the hot cooked rice. Top with a drizzle of juice from the drip tray.

Nutrition Facts Per Serving: 470 cal.; 20g protein; 20g fat; 50g carb.; 58mg chol.; 93g sodium

Grilled Chicken Legs with Latin-American Chipotle Sauce

Lunch & Dinner Entrées

SERVES 4
Prep Time: **40 minutes**
Cooking Time: **7 minutes**

2 cloves garlic, minced
2 tablespoons canola oil
1 ½ cups crushed tomatoes
2 tablespoons dark brown sugar
2 tablespoons molasses
¼ cup cider vinegar
2 tablespoons Worcestershire sauce
2 tablespoons chipotles in adobe sauce
¼ teaspoon ground allspice
8 skinless chicken legs
nonfat cooking spray

1. In a large saucepan set over medium heat, lightly brown the minced garlic in the oil. Add the tomatoes, brown sugar, molasses, vinegar, and Worcestershire, whisking to blend. Add the chipotles and the allspice. Whisk to combine.

2. Bring the sauce to a boil and reduce the heat to low. Simmer, uncovered, until the sauce is thickened, about 30 minutes.

3. Remove any visible fat from the chicken. Coat the grill with the cooking spray and preheat for 5 minutes. Place one-half of the sauce in a small bowl and brush the chicken with the sauce. Use the remaining sauce for dipping. Grill the chicken legs for 5 to 7 minutes, basting at least twice while grilling.

Nutrition Facts Per Serving: 148 cal.; 13g protein; 5g fat; 15g carb.; 45mg chol.; 216g sodium

As Seen on TV Fun Fact

According to research conducted by the Electronic Retailing Association, consumers trust infomercials more than they trust Congress, corporate executives, and used-car salesmen.

Lunch & Dinner Entrées

SERVES 4
Prep Time: **10 minutes**
Cooking Time: **9 minutes**

Grilled Lamb & Beefsteak Tomatoes

4 boneless lamb chops, about 6 ounces each
1 teaspoon fresh thyme, minced
1 teaspoon fresh parsley, minced
splash balsamic vinegar
¼ teaspoon black pepper
4 large, ripe beefsteak tomatoes, cored and thickly sliced

1. Preheat the grill for 5 minutes.

2. Place the lamb chops in the grill; dust with half of the thyme, parsley, vinegar, and pepper. Cook 5 to 6 minutes. Remove and transfer to a warm platter.

3. Add the tomatoes to the grill; dust with the remaining thyme, parsley, vinegar, and pepper. Grill 3 minutes, or until softened and warm.

4. To serve, mound the tomatoes over the lamb and serve while hot.

Nutrition Facts Per Serving: 263 cal.; 36g protein; 9g fat; 9g carb.; 109mg chol.; 125g sodium

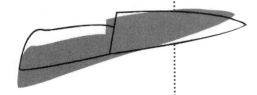

Grilled Parmesan Chicken with Angel Hair Pasta

Lunch & Dinner Entrées

SERVES 4
Prep Time: **10 minutes**
Cooking Time: **4 minutes**

2 boneless skinless chicken breasts
2 tablespoons extra virgin olive oil
3 cloves garlic, finely minced
2 tablespoons fresh parsley, finely minced
1 teaspoon ground oregano
1 teaspoon dried basil
¼ cup Parmesan cheese, grated
1 teaspoon black pepper, coarsely ground
½ teaspoon salt
nonfat cooking spray
10 ounces angel hair pasta, cooked al dente and drained

1. Remove any visible fat from the chicken. Slice the chicken thinly across the grain of the meat.

2. In a small bowl, combine the oil, garlic, parsley, oregano, basil, Parmesan, pepper, and salt.

3. Coat the grill with the cooking spray and preheat for 5 minutes.

4. Grill the chicken slices for 3 to 4 minutes or until fully cooked.

5. Place the pasta on a serving platter, pour the sauce over and toss well. Arrange the chicken slices on top and serve immediately.

Nutrition Facts Per Serving: 390 cal.; 21g protein; 11g fat; 52g carb.; 26mg chol.; 444g sodium

Grilled Salmon with Lemon-Basil Butter

nonfat cooking spray
4 salmon fillets, about 6 ounces each
1 teaspoon paprika
1 teaspoon sugar
½ cup low-fat margarine
1 teaspoon fresh basil, finely minced
2 tablespoons fresh lemon juice
1 tablespoon green onions, finely minced

1. Lightly coat the grill with the cooking spray and preheat for 5 minutes.

2. Place the salmon fillets in the grill and sprinkle with the paprika and sugar. Grill for 6 to 8 minutes, or until the fish flakes easily.

3. In a small bowl, blend the margarine, basil, lemon juice, and green onions. To serve, arrange each steak on a plate and top with a generous spoonful of the lemon-basil butter.

Nutrition Facts Per Serving: 418 cal.; 34g protein; 30g fat; 3g carb.; 112mg chol.; 234g sodium

Grilled Shrimp & Pepper Medley

Lunch & Dinner Entrées

SERVES 4
Prep Time: **10 minutes,** plus marinating
Cooking Time: **3 minutes**

1 red pepper, seeded and thinly sliced
1 green pepper, seeded and thinly sliced
1 small white onion, thinly sliced
1 teaspoon coarse black pepper
½ teaspoon salt
1 tablespoon extra virgin olive oil
1 tablespoon fresh lemon juice
1 teaspoon lemon zest
nonfat cooking spray
16 jumbo uncooked shrimp, peeled, deveined, tails removed

1. In a large bowl, mix together the peppers, onion, black pepper, salt, oil, lemon juice, and zest. Let stand for 10 minutes so flavors can meld.

2. Lightly coat the grill with the cooking spray and preheat for 5 minutes. Grill the shrimp for 1½ minutes. Place the peppers on top the shrimp and grill an additional 1½ minutes, or until the vegetables are tender and the shrimp are pink throughout.

Nutrition Facts Per Serving: 91 cal.; 7g protein; 4g fat; 8g carb.; 42mg chol.; 334g sodium

Lunch & Dinner Entrées

SERVES 4

Prep Time: **10 minutes**
Cooking Time: **7 minutes**

Lemon-Orange Rubbed Chicken Breasts

2 tablespoons low-fat margarine
¼ cup fresh lemon juice
¼ cup light brown sugar, packed
¼ cup frozen orange juice concentrate
1 teaspoon orange zest, minced
½ teaspoon ground mace
½ teaspoon salt
½ teaspoon black pepper
4 boneless, skinless chicken breast halves
nonfat cooking spray

1. Combine the margarine, lemon juice, and brown sugar in a mixing bowl. Mix until smooth. Blend in the orange juice, zest, mace, salt, and pepper. Mix well. Cover the chicken completely with the lemon-orange rub.

2. Coat the grill with cooking spray and preheat for 5 minutes.

3. Grill the chicken for 5 to 7 minutes, or until no pink remains.

Nutrition Facts Per Serving: 191 cal.; 17g protein; 4g fat; 22g carb.; 41mg chol.; 381g sodium

Rosemary-Butter London Broil

Lunch & Dinner Entrées

SERVES 6

Prep Time: **10 minutes**

Cooking Time: **8 minutes**

nonfat cooking spray
½ cup low-fat unsalted margarine
1 clove garlic, minced
1 teaspoon paprika
1 tablespoon fresh rosemary, finely minced
1 teaspoon salt
2 tablespoons finely chopped green onions
1 teaspoon black pepper
1 ½ pounds beef London broil steak, 1 ½-inch thick

1. Coat the grill with cooking spray and preheat for 5 minutes.

2. In a small bowl, combine the margarine, garlic, paprika, rosemary, salt, green onions, and black pepper; blend well.

3. Remove any visible fat from the steak and grill for 3 minutes. Brush the butter-herb sauce over the steak and grill for an additional 4 to 5 minutes. As the butter sauce melts, it will run into the drip tray.

4. To serve, slice the beef thinly across the grain and arrange on a warm serving platter. Pour the melted butter sauce from the drip tray over the sliced beef.

Nutrition Facts Per Serving: 267 cal.; 25g protein; 18g fat; 1g carb.; 67mg chol.; 446g sodium

Smoky Barbecued Beef Burgers

2 tablespoons Worcestershire sauce
2 tablespoons bottled liquid smoke
½ cup tomato sauce
1 tablespoon brown sugar
1 tablespoon prepared mustard
½ teaspoon seasoned salt
¼ teaspoon ground black pepper
1 pound extra lean ground round beef
nonfat cooking spray
4 large hamburger buns

1. In a medium bowl, stir together the Worcestershire, liquid smoke, tomato sauce, brown sugar, mustard, salt and the black pepper. Add the beef and toss lightly without overmixing. Shape the mixture into 4 hamburger patties.

2. Lightly spray the grill with cooking spray and preheat for 5 minutes.

3. Place the patties on the grill and cook for 7 to 8 minutes, or to desired doneness. Lightly toast the buns under the oven broiler, if desired, and serve with condiments of your choice.

Nutrition Facts Per Serving: 405 cal.; 26g protein; 23g fat; 28g carb.; 78mg chol.; 682g sodium

"Some Like It Hot" Italian Sausage Burger

Lunch & Dinner Entrées

SERVES 6
Prep Time: **15 minutes**
Cooking Time: **8 minutes**

1 pound uncooked Italian turkey sausage
½ cup fresh or prepared salsa
1 to 2 teaspoons hot pepper sauce (optional)
¼ teaspoon ground black pepper
1 egg white
¼ cup seasoned bread crumbs
nonfat cooking spray
6 large sourdough buns
⅓ cup Jack cheese, shredded

1. Remove the sausage from the casings and place in a medium bowl. Add the salsa, hot pepper sauce, black pepper, egg white, and bread crumbs. Combine thoroughly, mixing with your hands. Shape the mixture into 4 patties.

2. Spray the grill with cooking spray and preheat for 5 minutes.

3. Place the patties on the grill and cook for 7 to 8 minutes, or until the burgers are no longer pink in the center.

4. Toast the sourdough buns under the broiler. Place the patties on the toasted buns and sprinkle Jack cheese over each.

Nutrition Facts Per Serving: 332 cal.; 15g protein; 24g fat; 19g carb.; 46mg chol.; 801g sodium

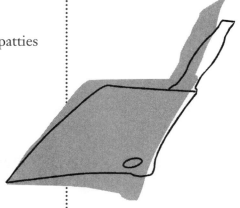

Lunch & Dinner Entrées

SERVES 4
Prep Time: **10 minutes**
Cooking Time: **6 minutes**

Spicy Asian Chicken with Chopped Peanuts

2 tablespoons peanut oil
1 tablespoon ground ginger
1 tablespoon Chinese five-spice powder
½ teaspoon red pepper flakes
½ cup finely chopped green onions
¼ cup low-sodium soy sauce
¼ cup rice vinegar
4 boneless, skinless chicken breast halves
nonfat cooking spray
¼ cup shelled and finely chopped peanuts

1. In a medium bowl, mix together the peanut oil, ginger, five-spice powder, pepper flakes, green onions, soy sauce, and vinegar. Blend well.

2. Remove any visible fat from the chicken. Coat the grill with the cooking spray and preheat for 5 minutes.

3. Place the chicken in the grill; cook 2 minutes. Spoon the sauce over the top of the chicken; cook an additional 3 to 4 minutes, basting occasionally, until the chicken is fully cooked and no pink remains. Serve topped with the chopped peanuts.

Nutrition Facts Per Serving: 234 cal.; 21g protein; 13g fat; 9g carb.; 41mg chol.; 583g sodium

Spicy Grilled Pork & Red Potatoes

Lunch & Dinner Entrées

SERVES 4
Prep Time: **10 minutes, plus marinating**
Cooking Time: **10 minutes**

4 pork chops, about 6 ounces each
1 pound small red potatoes, scrubbed
  and cut into small wedges
4 tablespoons prepared mustard
¾ teaspoon dark brown sugar
½ teaspoon prepared horseradish
¾ cup chili sauce
2 tablespoons cider vinegar
nonfat cooking spray

1. Remove any excess fat from the pork chops and place in a glass pan; place the red potatoes in a sealable plastic bag.

2. In a small bowl, whisk together the mustard, brown sugar, horseradish, chili sauce, and vinegar until blended. Pour half of the sauce over the meat.

3. Cover the meat; pour remaining sauce over the potatoes. Marinate both the meat and the potatoes for 2 to 4 hours.

4. Spray the grill with cooking spray and preheat for 5 minutes.

5. Place the potatoes on the grill and cook for 4 minutes. Push the potatoes to the sides of the grill and add the pork chops. Grill for 5 to 6 minutes.

Nutrition Facts Per Serving: 446 cal.; 37g protein; 23g fat; 23g carb.; 114mg chol.; 1712g sodium

Tex-Mex Steak Fajitas

Lunch & Dinner Entrées

SERVES 8
Prep Time: **10 minutes,** *plus marinating*
Cooking Time: **8 minutes**

½ pound beef flank steak
⅓ cup fresh lime juice
¼ cup prepared chili sauce
¼ cup vegetable oil
1 small white onion, chopped
¼ cup fresh cilantro, chopped
⅛ teaspoon chili powder
½ teaspoon ground cumin
½ teaspoon salt
½ teaspoon black pepper
1 green pepper
1 red pepper
nonfat cooking spray
8 low-fat, fajita-size flour tortillas
½ cup low-fat cheddar cheese
½ cup nonfat sour cream

1. Remove any visible fat from the steak. Cut the steak into very thin slices across the grain and place in a flat glass pan.

2. In a small bowl, mix together the lime juice, chili sauce, oil, onion, cilantro, chili powder, cumin, salt, and pepper. Pour mixture over the steak and refrigerate for 2 to 4 hours.

3. Remove the seeds and inner fibers from the green and red peppers and cut into thin slices.

4. Coat the grill with cooking spray and preheat for 5 minutes.

5. Discard the marinade and grill the steak for 3 minutes. Add the peppers over the top of the steak and grill for 4 to 5 minutes. To serve, fill warm tortillas with the meat and vegetables. Add cheese and sour cream as desired.

Nutrition Facts Per Serving: 281 cal.; 13g protein; 10g fat; 35g carb.; 17mg chol.; 825g sodium

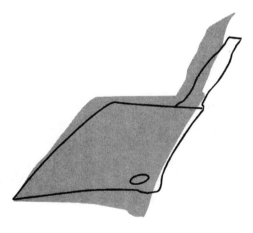

Zesty Dijon Beef Tri-Tip

nonfat cooking spray
½ cup low-sodium soy sauce
¾ cup balsamic vinegar
2 tablespoons extra virgin olive oil
2 tablespoons mustard
3 cloves garlic, minced
1 teaspoon pepper
2 habañero peppers, seeded
3 tabasco peppers, minced
2 pounds beef tri-tip roast

1. Coat the grill with cooking spray and preheat for 5 minutes.

2. In a small bowl, combine the soy sauce, vinegar, olive oil, mustard, garlic, pepper, and the habañero and tabasco peppers. Blend well.

3. Remove any visible fat from the roast and slice thinly across the grain. Place the slices of roast on the grill and brush with basting sauce. Grill 2 minutes and brush with sauce again. Grill an additional 3 to 5 minutes.

Nutrition Facts Per Serving: 296 cal.; 23g protein; 18g fat; 7g carb.; 74mg chol.; 1222g sodium

Enchilada Cheese Quesadillas

4 low-fat flour tortillas
½ cup enchilada sauce
1 cup pepper Jack cheese, shredded
2 tablespoons chopped green onions
3 tablespoons sliced black olives
1 tablespoon chopped fresh cilantro
nonfat cooking spray

1. Liberally brush 1 side of each tortilla with the enchilada sauce. Evenly divide the cheese among the tortillas, spreading the cheese on only half of each. Top each layer of cheese with green onions, black olives and the cilantro. Fold the empty half of the tortilla over the cheese mixture.

2. Spray the grill with cooking spray and preheat for 5 minutes.

3. Place one filled tortilla onto the grill and cook for 2 to 3 minutes, until lightly browned. Remove the grilled quesadilla and repeat with the remaining quesadillas.

Nutrition Facts Per Serving: 254 cal.; 13g protein; 11g fat; 29g carb.; 18mg chol.; 806g sodium

Snacks & Sandwiches

SERVES 4
Prep Time: **10 minutes**
Cooking Time: **8 minutes**

Grilled Portobello Mushroom Sandwiches

nonfat cooking spray
2 portobello mushrooms, thickly sliced
2 tablespoons extra virgin olive oil, divided
2 teaspoons balsamic vinegar, divided
¼ teaspoon ground black pepper, divided
½ teaspoon seasoned salt, divided
½ small red onion, thinly sliced
1 green bell pepper, thinly sliced
4 onion rolls, split
2 tablespoons chopped fresh Italian parsley

1. Spray the grill with cooking spray and preheat for 5 minutes.

2. Place the mushroom slices on the grill and drizzle with 1 tablespoon olive oil and 1 teaspoon balsamic vinegar. Sprinkle with half of the pepper and seasoned salt. Grill for 4 minutes.

3. Place the onion and green pepper slices on top of the mushroom slices; drizzle with the remaining oil and vinegar and season with the remaining pepper and salt. Grill for 3 to 4 minutes. Toast the rolls under the broiler and then evenly distribute the grilled vegetables and portobello mushrooms onto the rolls for each sandwich. Garnish with parsley and serve.

Nutrition Facts Per Serving: 202 cal.; 5g protein; 9g fat; 28g carb.; 0mg chol.; 226g sodium

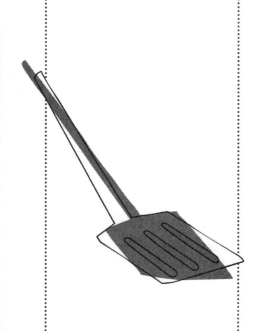

Summertime Fruit Skewers with Cinnamon-Sugar

Desserts

SERVES 4
Prep Time: **10 minutes**
Cooking Time: **3 minutes**

1 tart baking apple, peeled and cut into 1-inch chunks
2 plums, peeled and cut into 1-inch chunks
2 peaches, peeled and cut into 1-inch chunks
8 bamboo skewers (10 inches long), soaked in water
  for 20 minutes
3 tablespoons low-fat butter, melted
2 tablespoons sugar
1 teaspoon ground cinnamon
nonfat cooking spray

1. Thread the fruit onto the skewers, alternating the different fruits.

2. In a small bowl, combine the butter, sugar, and cinnamon until the sugar has dissolved.

3. Spray the grill with cooking spray and preheat for 5 minutes.

4. Place the skewers on the grill horizontally and brush each piece of fruit with the butter and cinnamon-sugar mixture. Grill the fruit for 2 to 3 minutes.

Nutrition Facts Per Serving: 147 cal.; 1g protein; 5g fat; 28g carb.; 15mg chol.; 53g sodium

Chapter 3

Jack LaLanne Power Juicer

J ack LaLanne, television's first fitness guru, has been preaching and teaching people how to add years to their lives—and life to their years— for more than half a century, and he's still going strong.

But Jack didn't start out that way. At the tender age of 13, he was a self-confessed "sugar-holic" who suffered from frequent headaches and violent outbursts. At age 15, he attended a health lecture that changed his life and set him on the path to health and fitness. After that, he practically invented the American health industry. In fact, he opened America's very first health club in 1936 and hosted the nation's longest running exercise program.

Jack's nearing age 90, but he's showing no signs of slowing down. He gets up at 5:00 A.M. every morning and works out for two hours.

"I'm going to live to be 150 years old," Jack told the audience on Hollywood Boulevard at a ceremony during which he was awarded his own star on the Walk of Fame. "Stick around and find out."

We won't guarantee that Jack's Power Juicer will help you live that long, but we will vouch for the fact that fresh juices are packed with health-giving vitamins and minerals—and that definitely can't hurt.

The Beat Goes On

Beverages

SERVES 1
Prep Time: **10 minutes**
Cooking Time: **None**

4 medium carrots
2 stalks celery
1 beet, with greens

Place all ingredients into the Power Juicer chute and push through with the plunger.

Nutrition Facts Per Serving: 172 cal.; 5g protein; <1g fat; 40g carb.; 12g fiber; 0mg chol.; 234g sodium

Carrot Cake Juice

Beverages

SERVES 1
Prep Time: **10 minutes**
Cooking Time: **None**

4 large carrots
¼ pineapple, skin removed and cut to fit into juicer chute
1 golden delicious apple
ground cinnamon, to taste
ground cardamom, to taste

Place all ingredients into the Power Juicer chute and push through with the plunger.

Nutrition Facts Per Serving: 199 cal.; 2g protein; 1g fat; 87g carb.; 21g fiber; 0mg chol.; 201g sodium

Cool & Light Juice

Beverages

SERVES 1
Prep Time: **10 minutes**
Cooking Time: **None**

2 large cucumbers, peeled
2 large carrots, washed, topped, and tailed
1 sweet apple, washed and stem removed
½ lemon, peeled

Cut the cucumbers, carrots, apple, and lemon into pieces that will fit into the Power Juicer chute and push through with the plunger.

Nutrition Facts Per Serving: 199 cal.; 6g protein; 0g fat; 51g carb.; 13g fiber; 0mg chol.; 66g sodium

This recipe calls for a sweet apple. Here are some other sweet varieties that work well.

Cortland. Crisp, juicy, and sweetly tart.
Empire. Sweet and spicy.
Fuji. Sweet and tart.
Golden Delicious. Mild and sweet.
Ida Red. Sweet and tart.
Macoun. Honey-sweet flavor.
McIntosh. Crisp, juicy, sweet.
Red Delicious. Sweet and mild-tasting.
Winesap. Sweet and tart.

Energy Boost Juice

1 carrot, washed, topped, and tailed
1 celery stalk with leaves, washed
1 beet root with leaves and roots, washed
loose parsley leaves, washed and rolled
loose lettuce leaves, washed and rolled
loose watercress leaves, washed and rolled
loose spinach leaves, washed and rolled
3 tomatoes, washed and stemmed
salt, to taste

Place the carrot, celery, beet, greens, tomatoes, and salt into the Power Juicer chute and push through with the plunger.

Nutrition Facts Per Serving: 121 cal.; 59g protein; 2g fat; 27g carb.; 7g fiber; 0mg chol.; 440g sodium

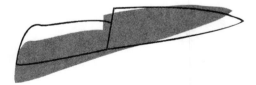

Fresh Apple Juice

3 large apples, washed and stems removed

Place the apples into the Power Juicer chute and push through with the plunger.

Hint: Mix sweet and tart apples for best flavor.

Variations: Add a carrot for a sweet difference and a vitamin boost. To spice up this juice add a sprig of mint or a slice of ginger.

Nutrition Facts Per Serving: 178 cal.; 1g protein; 0g fat; 51g carb.; 8g fiber; 0mg chol.; 8g sodium

Beverages

SERVES 1
Prep Time: **10 minutes**
Cooking Time: **None**

Could It Be the Juice? Part I

When Jack LaLanne isn't pitching his Power Juicer, he's performing incredible feats of human endurance on his birthday.

At age 40, wearing hand-cuffs, he jumped into the waters off Alcatraz prison and swam to San Francisco, just to prove he wasn't over the hill

Fresh Carrot, Apple & Ginger Juice

2 medium carrots, washed, topped, and tailed
1 crisp apple, washed, stem removed
1-inch piece (or more) fresh gingerroot, washed

Place the carrots, apple, and gingerroot into the Power Juicer chute and push through with the plunger.

Nutrition Facts Per Serving: 124 cal.; 2g protein; <1g fat; 32g carb.; 7g fiber; 0mg chol.; 54g sodium

Beverages

SERVES 1
Prep Time: **10 minutes**
Cooking Time: **None**

Beverages

SERVES 3
Prep Time: **10 minutes**
Cooking Time: **None**

Fresh Melon Combo Juice

½ cantaloupe, rind and seeds removed
½ honeydew, rind and seeds removed
½ watermelon, rind and seeds removed

Cut the cantaloupe, honeydew, and watermelon into pieces that fit into the Power Juicer chute and push through with the plunger.

Nutrition Facts Per Serving: 332 cal.; 6g protein; 3g fat; 77g carb.; 5g fiber; 0mg chol.; 41g sodium

Beverages

SERVES 1
Prep Time: **10 minutes**
Cooking Time: **None**

Fresh Orange Juice

5 large oranges, peeled

Cut the oranges into manageable chunks that fit into the Power Juicer chute and push through with the plunger.

Nutrition Facts Per Serving: 322 cal.; 7g protein; <1g fat; 81g carb.; 17g fiber; 0mg chol.; 7g sodium

Fresh Pear & Grape Juice

Beverages

SERVES 1
Prep Time: **10 minutes**
Cooking Time: **None**

2 pears, stems removed, cut into quarters
½ dozen seedless grapes

Place the pear and grapes into the Power Juicer chute and push through with the plunger.

Nutrition Facts Per Serving: 124 cal.; 1g protein; <1g fat; 32g carb.; 9g fiber; 0mg chol.; <1g sodium

Fresh Strawberry & Pear Champagne

Beverages

SERVES 1
Prep Time: **10 minutes**
Cooking Time: **None**

1 pint strawberries, washed and hulled
1 pear, stem removed
seltzer or dry, white champagne

Place the strawberries, pear, and seltzer or champagne into the Power Juicer chute and push through with the plunger.

Nutrition Fact Per Serving: 137 cal.; 2g protein; 0g fat; 33g carb.; 11g fiber; 0mg chol.; 3g sodium

The Green Drink

2 green apples
4 stalks celery
8 stalks bok choy
¼ pound spinach
1 bunch parsley

Place the apples, celery, bok choy, spinach, and parsley into the Power Juicer chute and push through with the plunger.

Nutrition Facts Per Serving: 207 cal.; 9g protein; 1g fat; 50g carb.; 14g fiber; 0mg chol.; 336g sodium

Could It Be the Juice? Part II

Jack LaLanne is known for his amazing physical accomplishments. Here are just a few.

- Completed 1,000 pushups in 23½ minutes
- Performed 100 handstand push-ups in 5 minutes.
- Towed 65 boats 2 miles. He was handcuffed and shackled to those boats, which were loaded with 6,500 pounds of wood pulp.

Love Potion

1 peach, pitted
1 cup grapes
1 cup strawberries
1 small apple, stem removed

Place the peach, grapes, strawberries, and apple into the Power Juicer chute and push through with the plunger.

Nutrition Facts Per Serving: 236 cal.; 3g protein; 1g fat; 60g carb.; 10g fiber; 0mg chol.; 2g sodium

Mango Surprise

Beverages

SERVES 1

Prep Time: **10 minutes**

Cooking Time: **None**

1 firm, ripe mango, pit and skin removed
1 kiwifruit
1 large carrot, tops and tails removed

Place the mango, kiwifruit, and carrot into the Power Juicer chute and push through with the plunger.

Nutrition Facts Per Serving: 162 cal.; 4g protein; 1g fat; 39g carb.; 11g fiber; 0mg chol.; 37g sodium

A Family Affair

Jack isn't the only one in the LaLanne family who's into health and fitness. His wife, Elaine, has written her own book, *Total Juicing* (Penguin 1992), which is loaded with recipes for juice and pulp, the bits of fruit or vegetable left over after juicing. One favorite is *Simple Salsa*. To prepare it, in a small bowl combine 2 cups tomato pulp, ½ cup onion pulp, and 1 teaspoon cilantro pulp. Mix well and serve with chips.

Papaya Surprise

1 papaya, skin and seeds removed, cut into spears
1 pineapple, top and skin removed,

Place the papaya into the Power Juicer chute and push through with the plunger. Repeat with the pineapple. Mix juices together well and serve.

Nutrition Facts Per Serving: 379cal.; 4g protein; 3g fat; 96g carb.; 13g fiber; 0mg chol.; 16g sodium

Rainbow Surprise

1 stalk celery
4 carrots, tops and tails removed
1 cucumber
1 yellow squash
1 zucchini
1 sweet apple, stem removed

Place the celery, carrots, cucumber, squash, zucchini, and apple into the Power Juicer chute and push through with the plunger.

Nutrition Facts Per Serving: 357 cal.; 9g protein; <1g fat; 87g carb.; 21g fiber; 0mg chol.; 201g sodium

Simply Carrot Juice

Beverages

SERVES 1
Prep Time: **10 minutes**
Cooking Time: **None**

4 large carrots, tops and tails removed
1 large stalk celery, with leaves

Place the carrots and celery into the Power Juicer chute and push through with the plunger.

Nutrition Facts Per Serving: 158 cal.; 4g protein; <1g fat; 37g carb.; 11g fiber; 0mg chol.; 126 sodium

Strawberry Special Juice

Beverages

SERVES 1
Prep Time: **10 minutes**
Cooking Time: **None**

5 large strawberries, hulled
½ pint raspberries
½ lemon, peeled, but with white pith remaining
sparkling mineral water or champagne

Place the strawberries, raspberries, lemon, and sparkling water or champagne into the Power Juicer chute and push through with the plunger.

Nutrition Facts Per Serving: 112 cal.; 2g protein; 1g fat; 28 carb.; 13g fiber; 0mg chol.; 219g sodium

Super Sunrise

Beverages

SERVES 1

*Prep Time: **10 minutes***
*Cooking Time: **None***

3 slices pineapple
½ orange, peeled
4 fresh strawberries, hulled
1 bunch red grapes

Place the pineapple slices, orange, strawberries, and grapes into the Power Juicer chute and push through with the plunger.

Nutrition Facts Per Serving: 271 cal.; 3g protein; 3g fat; 70g carb.; 6g fiber; 0mg chol.; 3g sodium

Triple Grape Drink

Beverages

SERVES 1

*Prep Time: **10 minutes***
*Cooking Time: **None***

½ pound red seedless grapes
½ pound green seedless grapes
½ pound purple grapes

Place the grapes into the Power Juicer chute and push through with the plunger.

Nutrition Facts Per Serving: 470 cal.; 4g protein; 4g fat; 118g carb.; 7g fiber; 0mg chol.; 13g sodium

Vitamin C Boost

Beverages

SERVES 1
Prep Time: **10 minutes**
Cooking Time: **None**

2 large oranges, peeled
2 large grapefruits, peeled

Place the oranges and grapefruits into the Power Juicer chute and push through with the plunger.

Nutrition Facts Per Serving: 350 cal.; 7g protein; <1g fat; 90g carb.; 17g fiber; 0mg chol.; 3g sodium

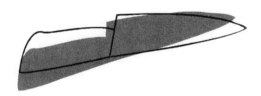

Chapter 4

Pasta Pro

People have been enjoying pasta for thousands of years, ever since it was invented in China, around 3000 B.C. However, it didn't come to America until 1789. That's when Thomas Jefferson brought a pasta maker home from France, where he had been ambassador. Jefferson loved pasta so much, he later designed and made his own pasta maker.

But macaroni—as it was almost universally known—didn't really take off in this country until the 1900s, with the arrival of hundreds of thousands of Italian immigrants.

Today, it seems everyone loves pasta. In fact, according to a survey conducted by the National Pasta Association, 77 percent of Americans eat pasta once a week and 33 percent have it *three or more times a week.*

With all that boiling and draining, you'd think that someone would have come up with a better way to cook pasta. That's where the Pasta Pro comes in. This inventive device combines the pasta pot with the colander, eliminating the need to dump a pot of scalding water into a strainer. Just lock the lid in place and pour out the water.

Part of what makes the Pasta Pro so ingenious is that it can handle more than just pasta: Use it to brown and drain ground meat for chili or to boil and drain potatoes for potato salad. It's so clever, Thomas Jefferson would be proud.

Lunch & Dinner Entrées

SERVES 6

Prep Time: **10 minutes**
Cooking Time: **15 minutes**

Chicken Chop Chop Pasta Bowl

2 cloves garlic, chopped

1 pound tubetini, ditalini, radiatore, pennette or other small pasta

1 pound boneless, skinless chicken breast, cut into small cubes

2 jars (26 ounces each) tomato basil pasta sauce

12 to 16 medium California ripe olives, coarsely chopped

1 package (8 ounces) shredded mozzarella cheese

1 cup grated Romano cheese

1. Add water and garlic to Pasta Pro set over high heat. Bring to a boil. Add pasta and chicken cubes to pot; cook until pasta is done (chicken cooks with the pasta).

2. Place lid onto Pasta Pro and turn to lock lid onto pot. Drain pasta; remove lid, and immediately return pot to heat. Add 1 ½ jars of the pasta sauce, the olives, and the mozzarella. Blend well and serve with generous amounts of Romano cheese and extra sauce.

Variation 1: Substitute Alfredo sauce for the tomato basil sauce.

Variation 2: Substitute 4 cups chopped fresh plum tomatoes for the tomato basil sauce.

Variation 3: Add frozen peas or other fresh or frozen vegetables to the pasta and chicken.

Nutrition Facts Per Serving: 523 cal.; 33g protein; 14g fat; 64g carb.; 8g fiber; 61mg chol.; 1270g sodium

Chili

1 pound lean ground beef
1 medium onion, chopped
2 cans (15 ounces each) spicy chili beans
2 cans (10 ounces each) whole tomatoes and green chilis
1 teaspoon unsweetened cocoa powder
¼ teaspoon ground cinnamon
1 cup grated cheddar cheese

1. Brown meat and onion in the Pasta Pro set over medium heat.

2. Place lid on Pasta Pro; turn to lock lid onto pot. Drain excess fat, remove lid, and return pot to heat.

3. Stir in beans, tomatoes, cocoa, and cinnamon. Cover, reduce heat, and simmer 10 to 15 minutes.

4. Remove lid, add cheese, and serve.

Nutrition Facts Per Serving: 602 cal.; 45g protein; 32g fat; 39g carb.; 12g fiber; 107mg chol.; 1580g sodium

Lunch & Dinner Entrées

SERVES 4
Prep Time: **15 minutes**
Cooking Time: **15 minutes**

Cocoa in chili? Well, yes. Unsweetened cocoa adds a complex, earthy flavor to chili. And no, it won't taste like chocolate.

Lunch & Dinner
Entrées

SERVES 4
Prep Time: **15 minutes**
Cooking Time: **12 minutes**

Down Home Macaroni & Cheese

1 ⅓ cups elbow macaroni
6 ounces processed cheese, shredded
½ cup shredded cheddar cheese
⅛ cup heavy cream
¼ teaspoon salt

1. Bring water to a boil in the Pasta Pro; add macaroni and cook until tender, 8 to 10 minutes.

2. Place lid on Pasta Pro; turn to lock lid into place. Drain macaroni. Remove lid from pot, reduce heat to medium, and return pot to stove. Immediately add the cheeses, heavy cream, and salt. Stir gently until the macaroni is well coated. Serve hot.

Nutrition Facts Per Serving: 349cal.; 17g protein; 21g fat; 23g carb.; 1g fiber; 65mg chol.; 843g sodium

Franks & Beans

Lunch & Dinner Entrées

SERVES 8
Prep Time: **5 minutes**
Cooking Time: **25 minutes**

1 package (16 ounces) frankfurters, cut into ½-inch pieces
2 tablespoons barbecue sauce
1 tablespoon dark brown sugar
2 cans (16 ounces each) baked beans

1. Place frankfurters in Pasta Pro over high heat with enough water to cover.

2. Place lid on Pasta Pro; turn to lock lid into place. Drain franks; remove lid from pot. Reduce heat to medium; return pot to heat. Add the barbecue sauce, brown sugar, and beans and cook until heated through, 10 to 15 minutes.

Nutrition Facts Per Serving: 332 cal.; 14g protein; 21g fat; 24g carb.; 6g fiber; 55mg chol.; 1218g sodium

Lunch & Dinner
Entrées

SERVES: 6
Prep Time: **10 minutes**
Cooking Time: **15 minutes**

Ham & Noodle Dinner

1 pound dry noodles
1 cup frozen peas (or other vegetable)
1 tablespoon butter
6 ounces diced cooked ham
2 cups heavy cream
1 cup grated Parmesan cheese

1. Bring water to a boil in the Pasta Pro; add noodles and peas. Cook according to pasta package directions.

2. Place lid on Pasta Pro; turn to lock lid into place. Drain pasta. Remove lid from pot, reduce heat to low, and return pot to stove.

3. Add the butter, ham, heavy cream, and Parmesan. Toss until well blended and serve.

Nutrition Facts Per Serving: 618 cal.; 24g protein; 34g fat; 54g carb.; 3g fiber; 127mg chol.; 416g sodium

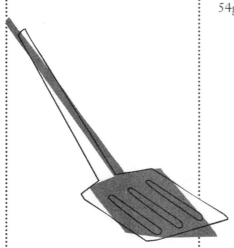

Home-Style Spaghetti with Baked Meatballs

1 tablespoon vegetable oil
¼ cup minced onions
2 pounds lean ground beef
2 eggs
¾ cup bread crumbs
½ cup milk
pinch salt
½ teaspoon pepper
2 teaspoons onion powder
½ teaspoon garlic powder
1 pound dried spaghetti
1 jar (26 ounces) prepared spaghetti sauce

1. Preheat oven to 400°F. Grease baking sheet lightly with oil.

2. Heat a small skillet over medium heat. Add 1 tablespoon oil and onions. Saute until tender, about 3 minutes.

3. Mix the beef, eggs, bread crumbs, milk, salt, pepper, onion powder, and garlic powder together in a bowl; add the sauteed onions. Mix until blended using a large spoon.

4. Shape beef mixture into 1- to 2-inch meatballs; place on prepared baking sheet. Bake until thoroughly cooked, 10 to 12 minutes.

5. Meanwhile, bring water to a boil in Pasta Pro set over high heat. Add spaghetti and cook according to package directions. Place lid on pot and turn to lock into place. Drain spaghetti. Remove lid; add sauce and stir to blend over low heat.

6. Divide spaghetti among six plates; top each serving with meatballs.

Nutrition Facts Per Serving: 599 cal.; 36g protein; 20g fat; 68g carb.; 5g fiber; 95mg chol.; 264g sodium

Old-Fashioned Beef & Noodle Casserole

Lunch & Dinner Entrées

SERVES: 4
*Prep Time: **20 minutes***
*Cook Time: **30 minutes***

1 pound lean ground beef
½ cup finely chopped onions
2 ¾ cups egg noodles
1 can (10 ¾ ounces) condensed tomato soup
pinch pepper
1 cup bread crumbs
1 cup grated cheddar cheese

1. Preheat oven to 300°F. Brown beef and onions in Pasta Pro set over medium high heat. Place lid on pot and turn to lock into place. Drain excess fat, remove lid, and transfer beef and onion mixture to a bowl.

2. Clean Pasta Pro and add enough water to cook pasta; bring to a boil. Add noodles and cook according to package directions. Place lid on pot and turn to lock into place. Drain noodles and set aside.

3. In a medium bowl, combine the soup and pepper. Stir into cooked beef. Add cooked noodles to the beef mixture, stirring gently.

4. Spoon beef and noodle mixture into a 9- by 13-inch baking pan. Top with bread crumbs.

5. Bake, uncovered, about 30 minutes. Top with cheese and return to oven until cheese is melted. Serve with salad.

Nutrition Facts Per Serving: 561cal.; 38g protein; 22g fat; 55g carb.; 3g fiber; 92mg chol.; 945g sodium

Pasta & Clam Sauce

8 ounces dry linguini, vermicelli, or angel hair pasta
12 little neck clams, washed and scrubbed
½ cup olive oil
5 cloves garlic, minced
½ cup dry white wine
1 can (10 ounces) fancy whole clams with their juice
¾ cup chopped fresh parsley
½ teaspoon each salt and ground black pepper
zest of ½ medium lemon
crushed red pepper, to taste
Parmesan cheese

1. Bring water to a boil in the Pasta Pro; add pasta. Boil until 5 minutes cooking time remains for pasta.

2. Add fresh clams to boiling pasta. Cook 5 minutes more. Discard any unopened clams.

3. Place lid on Pasta Pro and turn to lock lid into place. Drain pasta and remove lid. Reduce heat to medium high and return pot to stove. Immediately add the olive oil, garlic, wine, canned clams with their juice, parsley, salt and pepper, lemon zest, and crushed red pepper. Serve with Parmesan cheese.

Nutrition Facts Per Serving: 677 cal.; 43g protein; 33g fat; 45g carb.; 2g fiber; 76mg chol.; 314g sodium

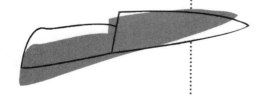

Pasta with Fresh Tomatoes

¼ cup olive oil

1 bag (10 ounces) fresh baby spinach leaves

6 plum tomatoes, each cut into 8 pieces

1 can (6 ounces) pitted black olives, drained

1 jar (6 ounces) marinated artichoke hearts (do not drain)

salt and pepper, to taste

2 teaspoons chopped fresh garlic

1 package (9 ounces) fresh fettuccine (from the refrigerator
  section of the grocery store)

⅓ cup freshly grated Romano cheese

1. In a large bowl, combine the olive oil, spinach, tomatoes, olives, artichoke hearts, and salt and pepper. Toss gently; set aside.

2. Place water and garlic in the Pasta Pro set over high heat.

3. Add fettuccine and cook according to package directions.

4. Place lid on Pasta Pro; turn to lock lid into place. Drain pasta, reserving ½ cup of the cooking liquid. Remove lid; add the spinach and tomato mixture and the reserved cooking liquid. Toss gently until spinach wilts. Sprinkle with Romano and serve.

Nutrition Facts Per Serving: 469 cal.; 13g protein; 26g fat; 49g carb.; 6g fiber; 3mg chol.; 858g sodium

Pasta with Pancetta, Pine Nuts & Shrimp

2 cloves garlic, chopped
8 ounces dry penne pasta
1 pound medium raw shrimp, shelled, deveined,
    tails removed, rinsed, drained
4 thick slices pancetta, diced
1 small red bell pepper
1 small green bell pepper
1 small yellow bell pepper
¾ cup whipping cream
1 cup mascarpone cheese
½ cup frozen peas, thawed
½ cup Parmesan cheese
2 to 3 fresh basil leaves, chopped
½ cup pine nuts, toasted
salt and pepper, to taste

1. Add water and garlic to Pasta Pro set over medium high heat; bring to a boil and add pasta. After 3 minutes, add shrimp. Cook until pasta is done and shrimp is opaque.

2. Meanwhile, saute pancetta in a medium skillet over medium heat until it begins to brown. Add the red, green, and yellow peppers; saute 3 to 4 minutes, or until pancetta is crisp. Turn off heat.

3. When pasta is done, place lid on Pasta Pro and turn to lock lid. Drain pasta; remove lid and return pot to heat. Immediately add the whipping cream, mascarpone, peas, Parmesan, and pepper mixture. Toss until ingredients are well blended and cheese is melted. If sauce is too thick, add more cream.

4. Remove pot from heat, sprinkle with basil and pine nuts and serve.

Nutrition Facts Per Serving: 621 cal.; 31g protein; 40g fat; 35g carb.; 3g fiber; 213mg chol.; 350g sodium

Pancetta is an Italian smoked bacon that is cured with salt and spices. Flavorful and slightly salty, pancetta comes in a sausage-like roll. In this recipe, you can substitute ham or bacon for the pancetta.

Pine nuts—also known as Mediterranean pine nuts, Italian pine nuts, Indian nuts, pignoli, and pignolia—come from the pine cone of the stone pine. They are torpedo shaped and have a light, delicate flavor. Pine nuts are available at most grocery stores. In this recipe, you may omit them all together, or substitute chopped walnuts.

Lunch & Dinner
Entrées

SERVES 6
Prep Time: **10 minutes**
Cooking Time: **15 minutes**

Pasta Primavera

1 package (16 ounces) penne or bow tie pasta
2 cloves garlic, chopped
1 cup frozen carrots
1 cup frozen peas
9 ounces frozen French-style green beans
6 ounces frozen pea pods
1 container (10 ounces) refrigerated Alfredo pasta sauce
¼ cup chopped fresh parsley or 1 tablespoon dried
2 teaspoons chopped fresh basil or 1 ½ teaspoons dried
¼ teaspoon fresh ground black pepper
⅓ cup fresh grated Parmesan cheese

1. Bring water to a boil in the Pasta Pro. Add the pasta, garlic, carrots, peas, green beans, and pea pods. Boil until pasta is done.

2. Place lid on Pasta Pro; turn to lock lid into place. Drain pasta. Remove lid from pot, reduce heat to medium, and return pot to stove.

3. Add the pasta sauce, parsley, basil, pepper, and Parmesan. Toss lightly and serve.

Nutrition Facts Per Serving: 432 cal.; 24g protein; 9g fat; 62g carb.; 6g fiber; 23mg chol.; 452g sodium

Pasta Rustica

Lunch & Dinner Entrées

SERVES 4
Prep Time: **10 minutes**
Cooking Time: **15 minutes**

1 onion

3 cloves garlic

12 ounces fresh pasta (from the refrigerated section of the grocery store)

1 can (15 ounces) pinto beans, drained and rinsed

1 ½ tablespoons extra virgin olive oil

3 tomatoes, chopped

2 ounces paper-thin slices proscuitto, cut into ½-inch strips

¼ cup grated Parmesan cheese

½ cup plus 1 tablespoon chopped fresh parsley, divided

1. Place water in the Pasta Pro set over high heat. Bring to a boil.

2. Meanwhile, process the onion and garlic in a food processor fitted with the metal blade until a paste forms. Set aside.

3. Add pasta to boiling water; cook according to package directions.

4. Place lid on Pasta Pro; turn to lock lid into place. Drain pasta; remove lid from pot. Reduce heat to low; return pot to heat.

5. Add the beans, garlic and onion paste, olive oil, tomatoes, proscuitto, Parmesan, and ½ cup parsley. Heat through and serve garnished with 1 tablespoon parsley.

Nutrition Facts Per Serving: 500 cal.; 22g protein; 11g fat; 72g carb.; 10g fiber; 79mg chol.; 1292g sodium

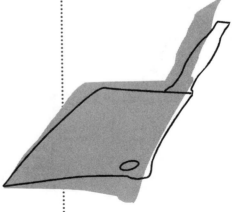

Warm Potato Salad

Side Dishes

SERVES 4
Prep Time: *25 minutes*
Cook Time: *15 minutes*

1 pound new red potatoes, washed, but not peeled.
1 cup diced onion
½ cup chopped celery
½ cup low-fat mayonnaise
2 tablespoons prepared mustard
1 tablespoon prepared horseradish
½ teaspoon salt
dash pepper

1. Place the potatoes in the Pasta Pro with enough water to cover. Bring to a simmer and cook until just tender, 10 to 15 minutes. Do not overcook. When potatoes are done, place lid on Pasta Pro and turn to lock lid. Drain pasta; remove lid and return pot back on heat.

2. In a small bowl, combine the onion, celery, mayonnaise, mustard, horseradish, and salt and pepper.

3. Pour dressing over warm potatoes in pot. Mix gently to blend. Serve warm.

Nutrition Facts Per Serving: 170 cal.; 3g protein; 3g fat; 34g carb.; 4g fiber; <1mg chol.; 681g sodium

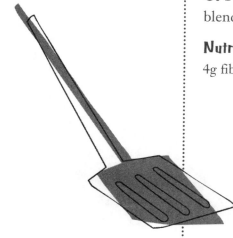

Perfect Pancake

The idea for the Perfect Pancake may seem new, but it might have been born on a Tuesday more than 600 years ago.

It was Shrove Tuesday in merry old England in 1400. The holiday marked the end of the period of celebration prior to Lent. The traditional Shrove Tuesday meal was a feast of pancakes, because preparing them would use up supplies of fat, butter, and eggs, all of which were forbidden during the time of fasting.

One particular Shrove Tuesday, an especially devout woman was busily preparing pancakes in her kitchen when she heard the shriving bell summoning her to confession. She raced to church, still wearing her apron, still holding her frying pan. Did the pancake fly out of the pan as she hurried to the church? The answer is lost to time, but that may have been when the idea for the Perfect Pancake was born.

These days, you probably don't run around holding a hot frying pan with a pancake in it. But if the need ever does arise, you can rest assured that the clever flat lid of the Perfect Pancake will keep your flapjack safe and sound. That's not the only advantage of the Perfect Pancake's design: If you have a hard time flipping flapjacks, you'll appreciate this clever contraption. Billed as the world's first spatula-free pancake maker, the pan let's you prepare delicious pancakes without leaving a mess on your stove. Let's eat!

Breakfast

MAKES 13⅔ CUPS; ENOUGH
FOR ABOUT 9 BATCHES OF 6
TO 8 PANCAKES EACH
Prep Time: **10 minutes**
Cooking Time: **None**

Light & Fluffy Pancake Mix

10 cups all-purpose flour
2⅔ cups instant dry milk
¾ cup sugar
¼ cup baking powder
2 tablespoons salt
1 vanilla bean (optional)

1. In a large bowl combine the flour, dry milk, sugar, baking powder, salt, and vanilla bean, if using.

2. Transfer mixture to a large airtight container and store in a cool dry place. Use within 6 months.

Nutrition Facts Per Batch: 645 cal.; 21g protein; 2g fat; 135g carb.; 4g fiber; 4mg chol.; 2328g sodium

Berry Pancakes

Breakfast

MAKES 8 LARGE PANCAKES
Prep Time: **5 minutes**
Cook Time: **40 minutes**

1 ½ cups Light & Fluffy Pancake Mix (page 106)
1 large egg
1 cup water
3 tablespoons vegetable oil
1 cup fresh or frozen strawberries, blackberries, or blueberries

1. In a large bowl, combine the Pancake Mix, egg, water, oil, and berries. Blend well and let sit for 5 to 10 minutes.

2. Preheat Perfect Pancake over medium heat.

3. Pour about ½ cup batter into the Perfect Pancake. Cook, with lid open, until edges are light brown and numerous bubbles appear on the pancake surface and hold their shape, about 4 minutes. Close the lid, flip over the pan, and cook until done, about 3 minutes more. Continue until all batter is used.

Note: Do not flip the pan while the batter is very loose.

Nutrition Facts Per Serving: 133 cal.; 3g protein; 6g fat; 17g carb.; 27g fiber; 25mg chol.; 270g sodium

Breakfast

SERVES 1
Prep Time: **5 minutes**
Cook Time: **2 minutes**

Here's how to make egg-ceptional eggs in your Perfect Pancake. Place 1 egg in the pan. Close the lid. Peek at the egg every 2 to 3 minutes. When the top appears to be solid, close the lid completely and flip the pan (away from the burner). Use the same flipping technique as you do to flip pancakes: When you're ready to flip the egg, close the lid. Holding the closed handle, quickly move the pan upward about 2 feet, flip the pan, and then move the pan quickly downward again. As you become more confident, you'll be able to cook more than 1 egg at a time.

Chick in a Basket

1 large egg
1 thick slice bread
1 teaspoon butter or margarine

1. Preheat Perfect Pancake over medium heat.

2. With a small juice glass or biscuit cutter, cut a hole in the center of the bread.

3. Spread half the butter on each side of the bread and place in the preheated Perfect Pancake pan.

4. Crack the egg into the hole in the center of the bread. Cook 1 minute (longer for a firmer yolk).

5. Close the lid and flip the pan. Cook 1 minute more; serve.

Nutrition Facts Per Serving: 253 cal.; 9g protein; 18g fat; 15g carb.; 1g fiber; 243mg chol.; 340g sodium

Light & Fluffy Apple Pancakes

Breakfast

MAKES 8 LARGE PANCAKES
Prep Time: **5 minutes**
Cook Time: **40 minutes**

1 ½ cups Light & Fluffy Pancake Mix (page 106)
1 large egg
1 cup apple juice
3 tablespoons vegetable oil
1 teaspoon cinnamon
1 apple, peeled, cored, and chopped

1. In a large bowl, combine the Pancake Mix, egg, apple juice, oil, cinnamon, and apple. Blend well and let sit for 5 to 10 minutes.

2. Preheat Perfect Pancake, with lid closed, over medium heat.

3. Pour about ½ cup batter into the Perfect Pancake. Cook, with lid open, until edges are light brown and numerous bubbles appear on the pancake surface and hold their shape, about 4 minutes. Close the lid, flip over the pan, and cook until done, about 3 minutes more. Continue until all batter is used.

Note: Do not flip the pan while the batter is very loose.

Nutrition Facts Per Serving: 152 cal.; 3g protein; 0g fat; 22g carb.; 1g fiber; 27mg chol.; 271g sodium

Perfect Pancake Flip Tip

Perfecting your flipping technique may take a little practice—but don't worry. Once you get the hang of it, it's simple. Here's some advice from the folks at Perfect Pancake.

When you're ready to flip the pancake, close the lid. Holding the closed handle, quickly move the pan upward about 2 feet, flip the pan, and then quickly move the pan downward again.

Breakfast

SERVES 6
Prep Time: **15 minutes**
Cook Time: **40 minutes**

Stuffed Chocolate French Toast

1 cup Light & Fluffy Pancake Mix (page 106)
1 tablespoon granulated sugar
2 eggs
1 cup low-fat chocolate milk
1 package (8 ounces) cream cheese, softened
½ cup chocolate chips
10 to 12 slices French bread, each 1 to 1½ inches thick
whipped cream (optional)

1. In an 8- by 8-inch baking pan, combine the Pancake Mix, sugar, eggs, and chocolate milk.

2. In a small bowl, combine the cream cheese and chocolate chips; mix well.

3. Cut a pocket into the side of each slice of bread. Stuff each slice with 1 heaping teaspoon of the cream cheese mixture.

4. Carefully dip stuffed bread slices into batter, coating both sides. Let sit 3 minutes.

5. Slide slices, one at a time, into the Perfect Pancake pan. Cook, with the lid open, 4 to 5 minutes over medium-high heat; close lid, flip, and cook another minute or so.

6. If desired, top servings with a dollop of whipped cream.

Nutrition Facts Per Serving: 890 cal.; 27g protein; 26g fat; 136g carb.; 7g fiber; 119mg chol.; 1687g sodium

To reduce the fat in this recipe by more than half, substitute non-fat cream cheese for the regular cream cheese called for.

Italian Luncheon Cakes

2 cups prepared biscuit baking mix
⅓ cup sharp cheddar cheese
⅓ cup Parmesan cheese
2 teaspoons each fresh parsley and fresh basil
½ cup each diced red pepper, diced green pepper, and
  chopped green onion
½ cup diced, cooked pancetta (optional)
¼ cup tomato sauce (not chunky style), plus extra for topping
1 cup half-and-half cream mixed with 1 tablespoon
  balsamic vinegar
2 eggs
Bel Paese or Brie cheese, to taste

1. In a large bowl, combine the baking mix, cheddar, and Parmesan, parsley and basil, red and green peppers, onion, and pancetta, if using.

2. In a separate bowl, stir together the tomato sauce, cream, and eggs. Stir egg mixture into baking mix and vegetable mixture until evenly moistened.

3. Preheat the Perfect Pancake over medium heat. Pour ⅓ cup batter into pan and cook 1 minute on first side and then 1½ minutes on the second side.

4. Serve hot with Bel Paese or Brie and extra warmed tomato sauce.

Nutrition Facts Per Serving: 341 cal.; 13g protein; 19g fat; 30g carb.; 1g fiber; 113mg chol.; 806g sodium

Pasta Pancake

Lunch & Dinner
Entrées

SERVES 4
Prep Time: **12 minutes**
Cook Time: **25 minutes**

8 ounces dry spaghetti
2 eggs
6 tablespoons Parmesan cheese, divided
2 cloves garlic, minced
fresh ground pepper, to taste
1 teaspoon olive oil
parsley, for garnish

1. Prepare pasta according to package directions; drain.

2. In a large bowl combine the eggs and 5 tablespoons Parmesan. Add the pasta, garlic, and pepper and toss until blended.

3. Pour oil into the Perfect Pancake and place pan over medium heat.

4. Toss pasta again; measure one-quarter of the mixture (about 1 cup) and spoon into the Perfect Pancake. Flatten into an even layer. Cook 5 minutes or until golden brown on the bottom.

5. Close pan and flip over. When golden on bottom, remove from heat. Top with remaining cheese and a sprig of parsley.

Nutrition Facts Per Serving: 293 cal.; 14g protein; 7g fat; 43g carb.; 1g fiber; 112mg chol.; 175g sodium

Spinach Pancakes with Goat Cheese

1 large egg
½ cup chopped spinach (if frozen, thawed and drained)
1 tablespoon grated onion
¼ cup reserved spinach liquid (from thawed spinach) or water
¾ cup Light & Fluffy Pancake Mix (page 106)
dash each salt and pepper
2 tablespoons virgin olive oil
10 ounces good quality goat cheese

1. In a medium bowl, beat the egg, spinach, and onion together.

2. Add the spinach liquid or water, Pancake Mix, salt, pepper, and olive oil. Mix well. Let stand 5 minutes.

3. Preheat Perfect Pancake over medium heat. Pour ⅓ cup batter into pan; cook 1 minute. Close pan, flip it, and continue cooking 1½ minutes on other side.

4. Place 1 tablespoon goat cheese in the center of each pancake and roll, crepe style.

Nutrition Facts Per Serving: 277 cal.; 13g protein; 16g fat; 21g carb.; <1g fiber; 58mg chol.; 535g sodium

Side Dishes

SERVES 4
Prep Time: **10 minutes**
Cooking Time: **15 minutes**

Potato Pancakes

3 large eggs
2 cups shredded hash brown potatoes
2 tablespoons all-purpose flour
1 ¼ teaspoon ground sea salt
¼ teaspoon ground pepper
¼ cup grated onion
1 package (8 ounces) sour cream
¼ cup chopped chives

1. In a large bowl, beat the eggs. Stir in the potatoes.

2. In a another bowl, combine the flour, salt, and pepper; stir into potato mixture. Stir in onion.

3. Preheat Perfect Pancake over medium-high heat. Pour ⅓ cup batter into pan and spread evenly. Cook 1 minute and then close lid, flip, and cook 1½ minutes more.

4. Serve with sour cream and chives.

Nutrition Facts Per Serving: 370 cal.; 10g protein; 25g fat; 30g carb.; 2g fiber; 184mg chol.; 824g sodium

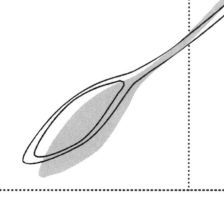

Double Chocolate Torte

1 quart heavy whipping cream, well chilled
4 tablespoons granulated sugar, divided
1½ cups Light & Fluffy Pancake Mix (page 106)
¼ cup premium unsweetened cocoa
1 large egg
1 cup chocolate milk
3 tablespoons vegetable oil
¾ cup miniature chocolate chips, divided
chocolate syrup, for garnish

1. In a chilled bowl and using chilled beaters, whip cream with 1 tablespoon sugar until soft peaks form. Set aside.

2. In a large bowl, combine the Pancake Mix, cocoa, 3 tablespoons sugar, egg, chocolate milk, oil, ½ cup of the chocolate chips, and ¼ cup water. Blend well. Let sit for 5 to 10 minutes.

3. Preheat Perfect Pancake over medium-low heat.

4. Pour about ½ cup batter into the Perfect Pancake. Cook, with lid open, until edges are light brown and bubbles appear on the pancake surface and hold their shape, about 4 minutes. Close the lid, flip over the pan, and cook until done, about 3 minutes more. Continue until all batter is used.

5. Arrange pancakes on a serving platter; top with some of the whipped cream. Continue adding alternating layers of pancakes and whipped cream, ending with the whipped cream. Top with remaining chocolate chips and drizzle with chocolate syrup. Serve immediately.

Note: Do not flip the pan while the batter is very loose.

Nutrition Facts Per Serving: 668 cal.; 8g protein; 56g fat; 40g carb.; 2g fiber; 192mg chol.; 336g sodium

For a less guilty pleasure, substitute a non-fat whipped topping for the heavy cream called for. It will reduce the amount of fat per serving from 56 grams to 12 grams.

Chapter 6

Ronco Showtime Rotisserie & Barbecue Oven

Whose name comes to mind when you think "infomercial?" It's probably Ron Popeil, the godfather of direct response television. And it's no wonder. Popeil invented and/or sold such As Seen on TV classics as the Veg-O-Matic, the Inside the Shell Egg Scrambler, the Food Dehydrator, and now, the Showtime Rotisserie & Barbecue Oven.

Ron got his start as a youngster, working for his father and Uncle, who were both in the biz of demonstrating and selling kitchen gizmos. In 1956, 21-year-old Ron hit the television airwaves pitching his father's Chop-O-Matic—the forerunner of the Veg-O-Matic.

In 1964 Ron set out on his own, starting Ronco Teleproducts with such products as the Dial-O-Matic and Slice-O-Matic. He eventually branched out beyond the kitchen with the famed Mr. Microphone, Buttoneer, and the Popeil Pocket Fisherman (which is still going strong).

Ron suffered a financial setback in the mid-1980s, but came roaring back in the early 1990s with the Electric Food Dehydrator and Beef Jerky Machine. The dehydrator sold hundreds of thousands of units and put Popeil back on top.

Ron's latest creation, the Showtime Rotisserie & Barbecue Oven has outsold every one of his other inventions, with sales almost reaching $1 billion. (That's a lot of chicken.)

And with ringing endorsements from sources ranging from *Good Housekeeping* magazine to Larry King, the Showtime Rotisserie & Barbecue Oven probably won't stop selling anytime soon.

Barbecue Chicken Salad

For the Tomato Barbecue Sauce
2 tablespoons vegetable oil
1 medium onion, chopped
3 cans (8 ounces each) tomato sauce
½ cup red wine vinegar
½ cup brown sugar
2 tablespoons Worcestershire sauce
½ teaspoon freshly ground pepper

For the Chicken
1 rotated Barbecue Chicken
½ cup chopped celery
½ cup chopped red bell pepper
¼ cup chopped red onion
½ cup mayonnaise
4 teaspoons Tomato Barbecue Sauce
4 lettuce leaves

1. For the barbecue sauce, heat the oil in a medium saucepan; saute onion until softened. Stir in the tomato sauce, vinegar, sugar, Worcestershire, and pepper. Simmer, uncovered, until thickened, about 30 minutes, stirring occasionally. Let cool, then cover and refrigerate for up to 2 weeks.

2. Shred the chilled rotated chicken and toss with celery, red pepper, and onion. Stir together the mayonnaise and barbecue sauce and toss with the chicken salad. Chill until ready to serve, up to 4 hours. Mound on lettuce leaves to serve.

Nutrition Facts Per Serving: 509 cal.; 7g protein; 33g fat; 51g carb.; 5g fiber; 26mg chol.; 349g sodium

Cajun Blackened Red Snapper

Lunch & Dinner Entrées

SERVES 4
Prep Time: **15 minutes**
Cooking Time: **20 minutes**

For the Cajun-Creole Rub

2 tablespoons paprika

1 tablespoon garlic powder

2 teaspoons dried thyme, finely crumbled

½ teaspoon dried oregano, finely crumbled

1 teaspoon cayenne pepper

1 teaspoon salt

1 teaspoon freshly ground pepper

For the Snapper

1 ½ pounds red snapper, cut into serving-size pieces

2 tablespoons melted butter

1. To make the Cajun-Creole Rub, in a medium bowl, combine the paprika, garlic powder, thyme, oregano, cayenne, salt, and pepper

2. Brush the fish with butter and dredge in the Cajun-Creole Rub to coat well.

3. Rotate the fish in the Flat Standard Basket for 15 to 20 minutes, or until just cooked through.

Nutrition Facts Per Serving: 242 cal.; 36g protein; 9g fat; 5g carb.; 2g fiber; 78mg chol.; 750g sodium

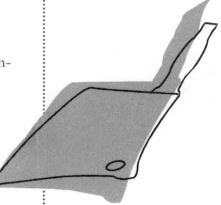

Lunch & Dinner Entrées

SERVES 4

Prep Time: **15 minutes**
Cooking Time: **18 minutes**

Filet Mignon with Roasted Garlic Sauce

2 whole heads garlic, roasted (see sidebar)
¼ cup (about) olive oil
1 cup red wine vinegar
3 shallots, finely chopped
2 cups chicken broth
4 beef tenderloin steaks (1-inch thick)
1 teaspoon crushed black peppercorns

1. Combine the vinegar and shallots in a small saucepan. Boil until nearly all the liquid has evaporated. Add the chicken broth and boil until reduced to about 1 cup.

2. Squeeze the garlic from the roasted cloves and puree in a food processor or blender. Pour in the broth and puree. Keep warm.

3. Press the pepper into both sides of the steaks and rotate in the Flat Standard Basket for 15 to 18 minutes, or until the meat reaches the desired doneness. Serve topped with roasted garlic.

Nutrition Facts Per Serving: 422 cal.; 33g protein; 21g fat; 30g carb.; 1g fiber; 78mg chol.; 580g sodium

To roast a head of garlic, preheat oven to 350°F. Remove papery outer skin of the garlic. Place garlic in an oiled baking pan; drizzle garlic with olive oil and bake until soft, 45 minutes to 1 hour.

Herb-Crusted Pork Chops

Lunch & Dinner Entrées

SERVES 6
Prep Time: **15 minutes, plus marinating**
Cooking Time: **25 minutes**

1 tablespoon dried basil
2 teaspoons dried sage
2 teaspoons garlic powder
2 teaspoons dried thyme
1 teaspoon dried rosemary
½ teaspoon dried oregano
6 (¾-inch thick) boneless pork chops

1. Combine basil, sage, garlic powder, thyme, rosemary, and oregano in a small bowl or with a mortar and pestle. Crush to combine well.

2. Wipe the pork chops with a paper towel and press herb mixture into all the cut surfaces. Rotate immediately; let stand up to 1 hour at room temperature, or refrigerate several hours.

3. Rotate the pork chops in the Flat Standard Basket for 20 to 25 minutes or until cooked through. If not brown enough, position the basket facing the heating coils and push the switch to the pause-to-sear position. Rotate 2 to 3 minutes on each side.

Nutrition Facts Per Serving: 195 cal.; 21g protein; 11g fat; 3g carb.; 1g fiber; 58mg chol.; 424g sodium

Lunch & Dinner Entrées

SERVES 6
Prep Time: 15 minutes
Cooking Time: 1 hour, 30 minutes

Italian Pork Loin with Garlic & Rosemary

4 cloves garlic, minced
½ teaspoon dried oregano, crumbled
½ teaspoon dried rosemary, crumbled
¼ teaspoon salt
¼ teaspoon freshly ground pepper
2 tablespoons olive oil
1 boneless pork loin (3 ½ to 4 pounds), trimmed and tied

1. Stir and mash together the garlic, oregano, rosemary, salt, pepper, and olive oil to make a paste. Rub all over the outside of the pork loin, covering as thoroughly as possible.

2. Rotate the pork roast on the spit rods for 1 hour 15 to 1 hour 30 minutes or until the internal temperature reaches 160°F on the instant thermometer. Remove roast, untie, and slice into ½-inch thick slices to serve.

Nutrition Facts Per Serving: 455 cal.; 62g protein; 21g fat; <1g carb.; <1g fiber; 200mg chol.; 246g sodium

Lemon Chicken Kebobs

Lunch & Dinner Entrées

SERVES 8
Prep Time: **20 minutes,** *plus marinating*
Cooking Time: **30 minutes**

4 skinless boneless chicken breast halves
1 zucchini, cut into 24 (1-inch) rounds
1 red bell pepper, cut into 24 (1-inch) squares
1 teaspoon grated lemon zest
3 tablespoons fresh lemon juice
1 ½ teaspoons sugar
¾ teaspoon dried oregano
salt and pepper, to taste

1. Cut each chicken breast lengthwise into 4 strips. In a large bowl, combine the chicken strips, zucchini, red pepper, lemon zest and juice, sugar, oregano and salt and pepper to taste in a large bowl. Toss to coat well. Cover and let stand 15 minutes.

2. Thread a zucchini, red pepper, and then a strip of chicken on a kebob rod; repeat and then finish with another zucchini and pepper. Repeat 7 more times. Rotate kebobs for 25 to 30 minutes or until the chicken and vegetables are cooked through.

Nutrition Facts Per Serving: 42 cal.; 7g protein; <1g fat; 2g carb.; <1g fiber; 17mg chol.; 20g sodium

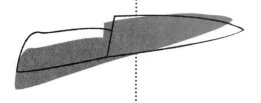

Lunch & Dinner Entrées

MAKES 10 TO 14
Prep Time: *10 minutes,*
plus marinating
Cooking Time: *45 minutes*

Mahogany Chicken Wings

¼ cup honey
3 tablespoons soy sauce
2 tablespoons hoisin sauce
1 teaspoon grated orange peel
1 clove garlic, minced
14 chicken drummettes or 10 chicken wings

1. In a food storage bag or a glass, plastic or stainless bowl combine the honey, soy sauce, hoisin sauce, orange rind, and garlic. Blend well.

2. Wash and thoroughly dry the chicken wings and add to the marinade. Seal the bag or bowl and refrigerate for 6 hours or overnight, turning occasionally.

3. Remove the wings from the marinade, reserving the marinade for basting. Rotate the chicken wings in the Flat Standard Basket for 45 minutes or until they are browned and cooked through, basting with reserved marinade during the last 10 minutes.

Nutrition Facts Per Serving: 121 cal.; 8g protein; 7g fat; 7g carb.; 0g fiber; 32mg chol.; 325g sodium

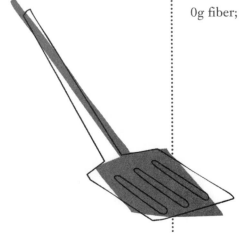

Marinated Top Sirloin Beef

Lunch & Dinner Entrées

SERVES 4
Prep Time: **15 minutes, plus marinating**
Cooking Time: **25 minutes**

½ cup ketchup

2 tablespoons soy sauce

1 tablespoon Worcestershire sauce

1 tablespoon brown sugar

1 clove garlic, minced

½ teaspoon chili powder

salt and pepper, to taste

1 sirloin steak (1 ¾- to 2-pound)

1. In a flat baking dish stir together the ketchup, soy sauce, Worcestershire, brown sugar, garlic, chili powder, salt, and pepper. Add the steak and turn to coat. Cover and marinate in the refrigerator for 2 to 8 hours.

2. Remove the steak from the marinade. Rotate the steak in the Flat Standard Basket for 15 minutes for rare or 20 minutes for medium. If not brown enough, position the basket facing the heating coils and push the switch to the pause-to-sear position. Rotate 2 to 3 minutes more on each side. Remove and slice thinly across the grain into thin strips.

Nutrition Facts Per Serving: 535cal.; 65g protein; 23g fat; 13g carb.; <1g fiber; 175mg chol.; 1057g sodium

Martini Shrimp

Lunch & Dinner Entrées

SERVES 8
Prep Time: **10 minutes, plus marinating**
Cooking Time: **15 minutes**

½ cup dry vermouth
¼ cup olive oil
¼ cup chopped onion
¼ cup lemon juice
2 tablespoons chopped fresh parsley
1 tablespoon white wine
Worcestershire sauce, to taste
2 cloves garlic, minced
½ teaspoon salt
½ teaspoon pepper
2 pounds extra-large shrimp, cleaned

1. In a shallow glass or stainless steel bowl stir together the vermouth, olive oil, onion, lemon juice, parsley, white wine, Worcestershire, garlic, salt and pepper. Toss the shrimp in the marinade. Cover and refrigerate for up to 4 hours.

2. Skewer shrimp on kebob rods and rotate for 15 minutes or until shrimp turn bright orange. Remove skewers from the gear wheels and slide the shrimp onto serving plates.

Nutrition Facts Per Serving: 210 cal.; 23g protein; 9g fat; 4g carb.; <1g fiber; 172mg chol.; 322g sodium

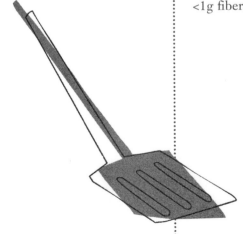

Pasta with Roasted Summer Vegetables & Feta Cheese

Lunch & Dinner Entrées

SERVES 4
Prep Time: **15 minutes**
Cooking Time: **20 minutes**

1 zucchini, sliced in half lengthwise

1 small eggplant, peeled and cut in half lengthwise

1 red onion, cut in half crosswise

¼ cup olive oil

2 cloves garlic, minced

2 tablespoons minced fresh basil

½ pound bow-tie pasta, cooked and drained

2 medium tomatoes, seeded and chopped

½ cup crumbled feta cheese

1. Prepare the vegetables. Stir together the olive oil, garlic and basil. Brush the vegetables with a light coating of the oil mixture. Rotate the vegetables in the Deep Basket 20 minutes or until very tender. Remove and coarsely chop.

2. Toss vegetables with hot cooked pasta, the remaining oil mixture, tomatoes and feta cheese. Serve immediately.

Nutrition Facts Per Serving: 430 cal.; 13g protein; 19g fat; 56g carb.; 6g fiber; 17mg chol.; 219g sodium

Lunch & Dinner Entrées

SERVES 6
Prep Time: **15 minutes**
Cooking Time: **40 minutes**

Poultry Chicken Cordon Bleu

6 skinless boneless chicken halves
1 tablespoon Dijon mustard
6 thin slices ham
6 thin slices Swiss cheese
2 eggs beaten with 2 tablespoons water
2 cups Italian seasoned bread crumbs

1. Wash and thoroughly pat dry the chicken breasts. Pound the chicken breasts lightly between two sheets of plastic wrap with a flat mallet until they are ¼-inch thick. Place the breasts, smooth side down, on a work surface and coat each with ½ teaspoon mustard. Top with a slice of ham and cheese. Fold in the sides and roll up the breasts. Secure with a toothpick.

2. Dip the chicken rolls in the egg mixture and then in the breadcrumbs to coat well. Rotate the chicken in the Flat Standard Basket for 35 to 40 minutes or until lightly browned and cooked through. Remove toothpicks and serve.

Nutrition Facts Per Serving: 359 cal.; 32g protein; 13g fat; 29g carb.; 1g fiber; 137mg chol.; 940g sodium

Roast Duck with Orange Sauce

Lunch & Dinner Entrées

SERVES 4
Prep Time: ***20 minutes***
Cooking Time: ***2 hours***

¼ cup orange marmalade
¼ cup fresh orange juice
2 tablespoons soy sauce
1 tablespoon Dijon mustard
1 clove garlic, minced
1 (4 to 4 ½ pounds) duckling
salt and pepper

1. In a small saucepan combine the marmalade, juice, soy sauce, Dijon, and garlic. Bring to a boil and simmer for 5 minutes.

2. Remove all fat from duck; wash and thoroughly dry inside and out. Prick duck skin in several places with a fork. Using an elastic food tie, truss the duck. Season inside and out with salt and pepper.

3. Rotate on the spit rods for 1 ½ to 2 hours or until the internal temperature reaches 170°F and the juices run clear. Brush the duck with some of the sauce about 15 minutes before the duck is done. Let stand 15 minutes before cutting into serving pieces. Serve with orange sauce.

Nutrition Facts Per Serving: 666 cal.; 84g protein; 27g fat; 16g carb.; <1g fiber; 349mg chol.; 945g sodium

As Seen on TV Fun Fact

Ron Popeil is famous for saying, "It slices, it dices," about his Veg-O-Matic, But it turns out that Ron never used that phrase during commercials for the gadget.

Lunch & Dinner Entrées

SERVES 4
Prep Time: *15 minutes, plus marinating*
Cooking Time: *15 minutes*

Salmon with Cucumber Sauce

As Seen on TV Fun Fact

Ron Popeil comes from a long line of pitchmen—his father and uncle demonstrated and sold cookware at fairs and stores in the 1940s. As a teen, Ron picked up the gift of gab, selling his father's products—one of which was the Chop-O-Matic—at street fairs and local five and dime shops.

For the Salmon
juice of 1 lemon
1 ½ pounds salmon fillets, cut into serving pieces

For the Cucumber Sauce
1 medium cucumber
½ teaspoon salt
1 ½ teaspoons white vinegar
1 small clove garlic, minced
1 tablespoon snipped fresh dill
1 cup plain yogurt
2 teaspoons olive oil

1. Drizzle the lemon juice over the salmon and rotate the salmon in the Flat Standard Basket for 10 to 15 minutes or until just cooked through.

2. To make the Cucumber Sauce, peel the cucumber, cut it in half lengthwise, and remove seeds. Grate the cucumber, place in a bowl, and sprinkle with salt. Refrigerate for 1 hour. In another bowl, stir together the vinegar, garlic, dill, yogurt, and olive oil. Drain the cucumbers and add to the yogurt mixture. Refrigerate for at least 4 hours before serving.

Nutrition Facts Per Serving: 386 cal.; 37g protein; 22g fat; 8g carb.; <1g fiber; 104mg chol.; 437g sodium

Skewered Shrimp & Scallops with Sage-Lemon Butter

Lunch & Dinner Entrées

SERVES 6
Prep Time: **15 minutes**
Cooking Time: **15 minutes**

For the Shrimp

3 tablespoons olive oil
grated zest of ½ lemon
2 cloves garlic
18 extra large shrimp, shelled and deveined
18 large sea scallops
2 tablespoons minced fresh parsley

For the Sage-Lemon Butter

1 tablespoon fresh lemon juice
1 teaspoon dried sage leaves
grated zest of ½ lemon

1. For the shrimp, stir together the olive oil, lemon zest, and garlic. Skewer the shrimp and scallops alternately on 6 kebob rods. Brush with the olive oil mixture. Rotate the kebobs for 15 minutes or until the shrimp turn pink.

2. To make the Sage-Lemon Butter, melt butter in a small saucepan. Whisk in the lemon juice, sage, and lemon zest. Set aside.

3. Transfer shellfish to a serving dish and pour Sage-Lemon Butter over. Garnish with parsley.

Nutrition Facts Per Serving: 125 cal.; 12g protein; 8g fat; 2g carb.; <1g fiber; 47mg chol.; 104g sodium

Lunch & Dinner Entrées

SERVES 4
Prep Time: **15 minutes**
Cooking Time: **25 minutes**

Turkey Burgers with Spicy Texas Rub

For the Spicy Texas Rub

6 tablespoons paprika

2 tablespoons ground black pepper

2 tablespoons chili powder

2 tablespoons salt

2 tablespoons sugar

1 tablespoon garlic powder

1 tablespoon onion powder

1 ½ teaspoons cayenne pepper

For the Turkey Burgers

1 ¼ pounds ground turkey

1 tablespoon Dijon mustard

1 tablespoon Worcestershire sauce

1 clove garlic, minced

½ teaspoon salt

¼ teaspoon black pepper

3 tablespoons Spicy Texas Rub

1. For the Spicy Texas Rub, in a medium bowl, combine the paprika, black pepper, chili powder, salt, sugar, garlic powder, onion powder, and cayenne.

2. For the Burgers, in a medium bowl, mix together the turkey, mustard, Worcestershire, garlic, salt, and pepper just until combined. Form into 4 patties.

3. Coat the patties with the rub. Rotate in the Standard Flat Basket for 25 minutes or until cooked through.

Nutrition Facts Per Serving: 260cal.; 26g protein; 13g fat; 10g carb.; 2g fiber; 112mg chol.; 2179g sodium

Corn on the Cob with Herb Butter

Side Dishes

SERVES 4
Prep Time: **10 minutes, plus soaking**
Cooking Time: **20 minutes**

4 ears fresh corn
½ cup butter, softened
1 green onion, minced
¼ cup minced fresh parsley
½ teaspoon dried tarragon
½ teaspoon dried marjoram
⅛ teaspoon freshly ground black pepper

1. Soak the corn in the husks in cold water. Place the corn in the Deep Basket and rotate for 20 minutes or until corn is heated through.

2. To make the Herb Butter, mash together the butter, green onion, parsley, tarragon, marjoram, and pepper. Serve corn with Herb Butter.

Nutrition Facts Per Serving: 325 cal.; 5g protein; 25g fat; 23g carb.; 3g fiber; 61mg chol.; 235g sodium

Side Dishes

SERVES 6
Prep Time: 15 minutes, plus marinating
Cooking Time: 25 minutes

Roasted Vegetable Skewers with Basil Marinade

For the Vegetable Skewers

1 red bell pepper, cut into 1-inch pieces
1 yellow summer squash, cut into ¼-inch slices
1 zucchini, cut into ¼-inch slices
16 cherry tomatoes
16 white button mushrooms, stems removed
8 green onions, cut into 1½-inch pieces

For the Marinade

½ cup olive oil
6 tablespoons balsamic vinegar
2 tablespoons minced fresh basil
2 cloves garlic, minced
salt and pepper, to taste

1. Prepare vegetables and place in a large bowl or food storage bag. Combine marinade ingredients and pour over vegetables. Cover and marinate 1 to 2 hours at room temperature.

2. Drain marinade and skewer vegetables on kebob rods. Rotate the skewered vegetables for 20 to 25 minutes or until vegetables are cooked through but still crunchy. Remove skewers from the gear wheels and slides the vegetables off onto serving plates.

Nutrition Facts Per Serving: 224 cal.; 4g protein; 19g fat; 14g carb.; 4g fiber; 0mg chol.; 17g sodium

Baked Cinnamon Apples

4 medium apples
¼ cup brown sugar
2 tablespoons toasted walnuts, finely chopped
½ teaspoon ground cinnamon
1 tablespoon butter
whipped cream

1. Core apples to within ½-inch of the base, leaving the bottoms intact. Cut off the stem top to fit back into the top of the apple.

2. Combine the brown sugar, walnuts, cinnamon and butter and pack into the apple. Fit the stem end back into the top. Rotate in the Deep Basket for 30 to 40 minutes or until apples are tender. Serve topped with whipped cream.

Nutrition Facts Per Serving: 223 cal.; 1g protein; 11g fat; 36g carb.; 5g fiber; 28mg chol.; 40g sodium

Fruit Kebobs with Grand Marnier Glaze

½ fresh pineapple, peeled, cored and cut into 1-inch wedges
4 bananas, cut into ½-inch slices
4 oranges, peeled and sectioned
12 large strawberries
1 cup sugar
1 teaspoon cinnamon, or to taste
6 tablespoons Grand Marnier

1. Thread the fruit evenly onto kebob rods, alternating pineapple, bananas, and oranges and placing one strawberry on the end of each.

2. Mix sugar and cinnamon and sprinkle over fruit. Rotate the skewered fruit for 15 to 20 minutes or until fruit is cooked through and lightly browned. Remove skewers from the gear wheels and slide the fruit onto serving plates. Sprinkle each serving with 1 tablespoon Grand Marnier and serve immediately.

Nutrition Facts Per Serving: 188 cal.; 1g protein; <1g fat; 41g carb.; 3g fiber; 0mg chol.; 2g sodium

Pineapple Wedges with Brown Sugar Sauce

Desserts

SERVES 4
Prep Time: **15 minutes**
Cooking Time: **10 minutes**

1 fresh pineapple
4 tablespoons butter
4 tablespoons brown sugar
2 tablespoons dark rum (optional)

1. Peel the pineapple and cut into eighths lengthwise. Cut off the core. Place the pineapple spears in the Flat Standard Basket. Rotate the pineapple for about 10 minutes or until warmed through and lightly browned.

2. Meanwhile, melt the butter and brown sugar in a small saucepan over medium heat. Add the rum, if desired, and stir to combine well. Drizzle the glaze over the hot pineapple and serve two spears per person.

Nutrition Facts Per Serving: 230 cal.; 4g protein; 12g fat; 28g carb.; 1g fiber; 31mg chol.; 122g sodium

Chapter 7

Turbo Cooker

Randall Cornfield needed something for dinner—fast. He had a breaded chicken breast, some white wine, and exactly 45 minutes.

Normally, Randall would have fried the breast and then baked it with the wine. But that would have taken too much time. So his choices were (a) find something else to eat; (b) just fry the chicken breast; or (c) fry the chicken, adding the wine to try and duplicate what he was going to do in the oven anyway.

Being a chef by training, he went with the third option. The challenge was to allow the wine to impregnate the chicken without it evaporating, as it normally does when cooking on a stovetop.

He first tried a flat lid, but the wine quickly evaporated and the pan went dry. He added some more wine and grabbed his wok lid. That worked better; less wine evaporated, but the pan still needed attention.

It wasn't perfect, but it was then that Randall had his "ah-ha" moment—understanding that it was the shape of the wok lid that made the process work better. The Steamfrying™ process and the Turbo Cooker were born.

The Turbo Cooker works because the cover allows a buildup of steam and heat which, from continued influx of steam, creates a convection action that speeds the cooking process and keeps more heat in the cooking unit.

Randall took his idea to a cookware manufacturer company and after 10 years of research and development the Turbo Cooker hit the market.

Breakfast

SERVES 6
Prep Time: **10 minutes**
Cooking Time: **20 minutes**

Gourmet Omelet Muffins

nonfat cooking spray
6 eggs, beaten
¼ cup green pepper, diced fine
¼ cup onion, diced fine
½ teaspoon salt
¼ teaspoon pepper
¾ teaspoon garlic powder
½ teaspoon parsley
⅓ cup grated low-fat cheddar cheese
6 lean breakfast sausages, 1-ounce each
3 cups frozen breakfast potatoes (in small cubes)

1. Spray the cups of a six-cup muffin tin with non-stick cooking spray. In a medium bowl, whisk together the eggs, green pepper, onion, salt, pepper, garlic powder, parsley, and ½ cup water. Pour mixture into muffin cups. Sprinkle each omelet with cheese. Place muffin pan onto steam rack.

2. Place sausages and ½ cup water into base; place steam rack into position. Cover (valve closed); cook on MEDIUM-HIGH heat 5 minutes. Add additional ⅓ cup water; flip sausages. Replace steam rack and cover (valve closed) 2 minutes.

3. Reduce heat to MEDIUM. Flip sausages, add ⅓ cup water, and replace steam rack. Cover (valve closed) 3 minutes.

4. Add 2 tablespoons water; stir to coat sausages. Remove sausages and transfer to either side of muffin pan (on the steam rack). Clean out pan; place potatoes in base; add ⅓ cup water. Replace steam rack, cover (valve closed), cook 5 minutes.

5. Add ¼ cup water; flip potatoes, replace steam rack and cover (valve closed) 3 minutes. Add remaining ¼ cup water. Replace steam rack; cover (valve closed) 2 minutes. Turn off heat; serve.

Nutrition Facts Per Serving: 187 cal.; 11g protein; 9g fat; 15g carb.; 1g fiber; 198mg chol.

Sausage Breakfast Pizza

½ pound precooked breakfast or kielbasa sausage, sliced
4 eggs, beaten
1 pound frozen shredded hash browns
salt and pepper, to taste
½ cup grated low-fat cheese

1. Place sausage rings in pan on MEDIUM heat, stirring until lightly browned. Remove from pan and wipe out any oil.

2. Place Turbo Cooker on HIGH heat. Add ½ cup water. Spread hash browns evenly over bottom; cover (valve closed) and cook 6 minutes.

3. Remove cover; turn potatoes and season with salt and pepper. Pour eggs over potatoes; sprinkle with cheese, and arrange sausage slices on top. Reduce heat to MEDIUM. Cover and cook 6 minutes.

4. To serve, slide pizza onto plate and cut into 6 wedges.

Nutrition Facts Per Serving: 238 cal.; 13g protein; 18g fat; 15g carb.; 1g fiber; 151mg chol.

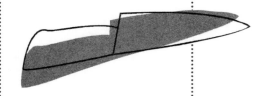

Beef Moussaka

Lunch & Dinner Entrées

SERVES 4
Prep Time: **15 minutes**
Cooking Time: **24 minutes**

1 ¼ teaspoon salt, divided
¼ teaspoon nutmeg
1 cup light ricotta cheese
2 cups skim milk
¼ cup all-purpose flour
3 eggplants, each cut lengthwise in 4 slices (12 slices total)
1 ½ teaspoons vegetable oil, divided
1 teaspoon pepper, divided
1 pound 98% lean ground beef
1 onion, diced
1 tablespoon tomato paste
¼ teaspoon cinnamon
⅓ cup low-fat grated mozzarella cheese
¼ cup low-fat grated Parmesan cheese

1. Place ¼ teaspoon salt, nutmeg, ricotta, milk, and flour into Turbo Cooker base. Cover (valve closed) and cook on MEDIUM heat 4 minutes. Whisk mixture until creamy, and then pour into a bowl and let cool.

2. Place 4 eggplant slices, ½ teaspoon oil, and ¼ cup water into the Turbo Cooker base. Cover (valve closed) and cook on HIGH heat 2 minutes.

3. Turn eggplant, sprinkle with ¼ teaspoon salt, and ¼ teaspoon pepper. Cover (valve closed) 1 minute.

4. Place eggplant onto steam rack and place another 4 slices onto base. Repeat steps 1 and 2. Repeat until all the eggplant slices have been cooked.

5. Clean base with paper towel. Place meat, onion, and ¼ cup water into base and place rack in position. Cover (valve closed) 3 minutes.

To reheat half the portion, place leftover food and ¼ cup water into base. Cover (valve closed) and cook on MEDIUM-HIGH heat 3 minutes. Reduce heat to MEDIUM; add 2 tablespoons water. Cover (valve closed) 3 minutes. Turn off heat and let stand for 1 minute.

6. Reduce heat to MEDIUM-HIGH. Crush meat with a potato masher; stir in tomato paste, cinnamon, remaining ¼ teaspoon pepper and ¼ teaspoon salt. Place rack in position; cover (valve closed) 3 minutes.

7. Reduce heat to MEDIUM-LOW. Remove all but 1 layer of meat sauce from base, then place 1 layer of eggplant on top of meat. Continue layering, ending with eggplant. Top with mozzarella, then cheese sauce, and Parmesan. Cover (valve closed) 5 minutes. Turn off heat; let sit 3 minutes before serving.

Nutrition Facts Per Serving: 487 cal.; 44g protein; 17g fat; 41g carb.; 9g fiber; 92mg chol.; 110mg sodium

Chef Randall's Oh-So-Easy Chicken Pot Pie

Lunch & Dinner Entrées

SERVES 6
Prep Time: **12 minutes**
Cooking Time: **14 minutes**

1 pound skinless, boneless chicken breasts, cut into
    ¼-inch cubes
¾ teaspoon salt
½ teaspoon granulated garlic
¼ teaspoon black pepper
1 teaspoon paprika (optional)
1 can (10 ounces) 98% fat-free cream of chicken soup
2 cups low-fat or 1% milk
2 heads broccoli, cut in small pieces
1 cup frozen peas
12 ready-to-use puff pastry shells (if using frozen,
    prepare according to package directions)
1 cup finely diced onion
½ cup white wine or chicken broth, divided
8 ounces mushrooms, cut in small pieces
½ cup finely diced carrot
3 tablespoons all-purpose flour

1. Season chicken with the salt, granulated garlic, pepper, and paprika, if using. In a small bowl, mix soup with milk. Place broccoli and peas onto vegetable rack. Remove and reserve tops of pastry shells; place open shells onto steam rack.

2. Place chicken and onion into base; add ¼ cup wine (or water). Cover (valve closed); cook on HIGH heat 3 minutes.

3. Add mushrooms and carrot. Stir in remaining ¼ cup wine (or water). Cover (valve open) 2 minutes. Stir in soup mixture and place vegetable rack into position. Cover (valve closed) 5 minutes.

4. Reduce heat to MEDIUM-HIGH. Sprinkle flour evenly over chicken and vegetables. Stir and cover (valve open) 2 minutes.

5. Reduce heat to MEDIUM-LOW. Stir chicken and soup into base. Place vegetable rack on top of steam rack and lock both racks into position. Cover (valve closed) 2 minutes. Turn off heat, stir, and serve (2 shells per serving). Fill each shell with mixture; top with reserved shell tops. Spoon more of the mixture onto the shells. Garnish with peas and serve with broccoli.

Nutrition Facts Per Serving: 179 cal.; 35g protein; 35g fat; 66g carb.; 9g fiber; 48mg chol.

To preheat half the leftovers, place chicken and sauce into the base, vegetables on the vegetable rack, and pastry onto steam rack. Turn heat to MEDIUM-HIGH. Stir ¼ cup water into base and place vegetable rack into position. Cover (valve closed) 4 minutes. Reduce heat to MEDIUM. Stir and place steam rack on top of vegetable rack and both racks into position; cover and cook 2 minutes before serving.

Clam Chowder

Lunch & Dinner Entrées

SERVES 8
Prep Time: **15 minutes**
Cooking Time: **20 minutes**

½ cup diced celery, for garnish
1 cup diced potatoes
2 cans (5 ounces each) clams
1 onion, diced
4 cups cubed potatoes
2 tablespoons low-sodium vegetable bouillon concentrate
½ teaspoon each salt and thyme
¼ teaspoon pepper
1 can (10 ounces) low-sodium cream of mushroom soup.
1 cup 1% milk
½ cup diced leeks, for garnish
fresh clams, washed, for garnish

1. Place the celery, diced potatoes, and canned clams onto vegetable rack. Set aside.

2. Place diced onion into base with ¼ cup water. Cover (valve closed) and cook on HIGH heat 3 minutes.

3. Add the cubed potatoes and 4 cups water. Cover (valve closed) 8 minutes.

4. Place rack into position; cover (valve closed) 5 minutes.

5. Stir in 1 cup water and vegetable bouillon. Place rack into position; cover (valve open) 4 minutes.

6. Place contents of rack into a bowl; set aside. Place the contents of the base into blender; process until mixture reaches desired consistency. Return mixture to base, stir in salt, pepper, thyme, milk, and soup. Reheat 3 to 4 minutes. Add the clams and serve garnished with celery, leeks, diced potatoes, and fresh clams.

Nutrition Facts Per Serving: 151 cal.; 8g protein; 2g fat; 26g carb.; 2g fiber; 13mg chol.; 461mg sodium

To reheat half the portion, place soup into base. turn to MEDIUM heat, cover (valve closed) for 2 to 3 minutes. Stir twice during reheating. Turn off heat and let stand 1 minute before serving.

Lunch & Dinner Entrées

SERVES 8

Prep Time: **10 minutes**
Cooking Time: **18 minutes**

Cream of Chicken with Dumplings

2 cups light Bisquick

1 ¾ cups skim milk, divided

2 tablespoons all-purpose flour

2 tablespoons cornstarch

3 tablespoons low-sodium chicken bouillon concentrate

2 carrots, diced

1 skinless, boneless chicken breast, cubed

½ onion, diced

½ teaspoon salt

¼ teaspoon pepper

½ teaspoon granulated garlic

1. For the dumplings, in a bowl, mix together the Bisquick with ½ cup water and ¾ cup milk. Set aside. In another bowl, mix together the flour, cornstarch, bouillon, and 1 ½ cups water until well blended. Place carrots on rack.

2. Place chicken, onion, and ¼ cup water into Turbo Cooker base. Cover (valve closed) and cook on HIGH heat 3 minutes.

3. Stir in 2 ½ cups water. Cover (valve closed) 6 minutes.

4. Reduce heat to MEDIUM; stir in the flour mixture and remaining 1 cup milk. Place rack into position and cover (valve closed) 4 minutes.

5. Stir in the salt, pepper, granulated garlic, and remaining 1 cup water. Gently spoon dumplings, 1 at a time, into the soup. Place rack into position, cover (valve closed) 5 minutes. Let sit 2 minutes before serving. Sprinkle carrots over the dumplings before serving.

Nutrition Facts Per Serving: 150 cal.; 7g protein; 2g fat; 26g carb.; 1g fiber; 10mg chol.; 476mg sodium

To reheat half the portion, place the soup and dumplings into the base; turn heat to MEDIUM and cover (valve closed) 3 to 4 minutes. Stir twice while the soup is reheating. Turn off heat and let sit 1 minute before serving.

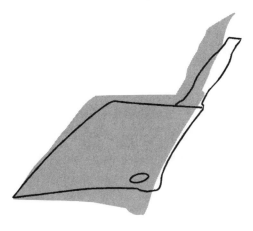

Fettuccine Seafood à la St. Jacques

3 teaspoons cornstarch
1 package (12 ounces) fettuccine, broken in half
1 teaspoon salt, divided
1 teaspoon oil
3 shallots, diced
8 ounces shrimp
1 cup scallops
3 teaspoons crushed fresh garlic
¼ cup white wine
½ cup half-and-half
¼ cup 2% milk
½ cup fresh or imitation crabmeat
½ teaspoon pepper
½ cup low-fat grated mozzarella
2 tablespoons chopped fresh parsley

1. In a small bowl, whisk together the cornstarch with 2 tablespoons water and set aside.

2. Place the fettuccine, ½ teaspoon salt, oil, and 3 ½ cups water into the Turbo Cooker base. Cover (valve open) and cook on HIGH heat 6 minutes.

3. Using a spatula, separate pasta and pour into a bowl; place bowl onto steam rack. Place shallots and shrimp onto base with ¼ cup water. Place rack into position. Cover (valve closed) 2 minutes.

4. Reduce heat to MEDIUM. Add scallops and garlic; place rack into position. Cover (valve closed) 1 minute.

5. Deglaze pan with the wine. Stir in the half-and-half, milk, cornstarch and water mixture, crabmeat, pepper, and remaining salt. Place rack into position. Cover (valve closed) 2 minutes.

6. Sprinkle cheese on top of seafood. Place rack into position and cover (valve closed) 1 minute. Drain pasta; transfer to plates and serve topped with seafood mixture. Garnish with parsley.

Variation: For a sharper flavor, use Swiss cheese.

Nutrition Facts Per Serving: 529 cal.; 37g protein; 9g fat; 72g carb.; 4g fiber; 125mg chol.

To reheat half the portion, place the leftover food into the base; turn heat to MEDIUM-HIGH. Add ¼ cup water; cover (valve closed) and cook 1 to 2 minutes. Reduce heat to MEDIUM. Stir and continue cooking 1 to 2 minutes. Turn off heat and let stand 1 minute before serving.

Fillet of Sole Marie Louise

1 cup all-purpose flour
½ teaspoon paprika
4 fillet of sole, 7 ounces each
4 cups fresh green beans, tips removed
3 cups thinly sliced potatoes
¾ teaspoon salt, divided
1 teaspoon unsalted butter
3 shallots, diced
8 ounces sliced mushrooms
2 tomatoes, diced
¼ teaspoon pepper
½ teaspoon granulated garlic
¼ teaspoon canola oil

1. In a bowl, combine the flour and paprika; pass the fish through the mixture. Place the beans on the steam rack.

2. Place potatoes, ½ teaspoon salt, and 2 cups water into base. Cover (valve closed) and cook on HIGH heat 6 minutes.

3. Drain the potatoes and place them on the steam rack with the green beans. Place the butter, shallots, mushrooms, and ¼ cup water into base; place rack in position. Cover (valve closed) 3 minutes.

4. Stir in tomatoes, pepper, granulated garlic, and remaining ¼ teaspoon salt and place rack in position. Cover (valve closed) 3 minutes.

5. Reduce heat to MEDIUM. Transfer the cooked vegetables to a bowl and place bowl on rack. Clean base with paper towel. Place fish in base with ¼ cup water; place rack in position. Cover (valve closed) 2 minutes.

6. Using a spatula, turn fish, then add oil. Place rack in position (valve closed) 2 minutes. Turn off heat; let sit 2 minutes before serving.

Nutrition Facts Per Serving: 381 cal.; 44g protein; 5g fat; 42g carb.; 6g fiber; 98mg chol.; 610g sodium

To reheat half the portion, place the leftover food and ⅓ cup water into base. Cover (valve closed) and cook on MEDIUM-HIGH heat for 2 minutes. Reduce heat to MEDIUM. Add 1 tablespoon water. Cover (valve closed) 4 minutes.

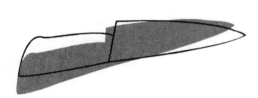

Grilled Salmon Steak

2 tablespoons or more Dijon mustard, to taste
½ cup skim milk
½ tablespoon cornstarch
½ teaspoon salt
¼ teaspoon pepper
½ teaspoon garlic powder
½ onion, diced
1 cup brown rice, rinsed
2 teaspoons low-sodium vegetable bouillon concentrate
1 teaspoon crushed fresh garlic
2 large slices salmon, each cut in half
3 cups broccoli, cut in small pieces
¼ cup white wine

1. In a bowl, mix the mustard, milk, cornstarch, salt, pepper, and garlic powder. Set aside for step 6.

2. Place diced onions, rice and 3 cups water into base. Cover (valve open) and cook on HIGH heat for 14 minutes.

3. Stir in the vegetable bouillon and fresh garlic. Transfer rice to a bowl, cover with aluminum foil, and place bowl on rack. Clean base with paper towels. Transfer salmon slices to base, add ¼ cup water, and cover (valve close) for 3 minutes.

4. Turn the salmon and add ⅓ cup water. Add the broccoli to rack and place rack into position. Cover (valve closed) for 3 minutes.

5. Reduce heat to MEDIUM. Gently move the salmon slices and add the wine. Place rack into position, and cover (valve closed) for 1 minute.

6. Stir in Dijon mustard mixture. Place rack into position and cover (valve closed) for 2 minutes.

7. Transfer the salmon to a serving plate and pour sauce over it. Serve with rice and broccoli on the side.

Nutrition Facts Per Serving: 388 cal.; 25g protein; 12g fat; 46g carb.; 4g fiber; 51mg chol.; 715mg sodium

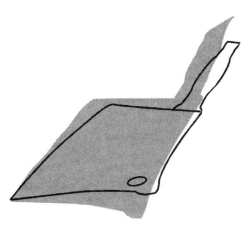

To reheat half the portion, place leftover food into base with salmon on steam rack. Turn to HIGH. Add ⅓ cup water into base, cover (valve closed) 4 minutes. Reduce heat to MEDIUM-HIGH, stir and cover for 3 minutes. Reduce heat to MEDIUM, stir and cover for 2 minutes. Turn off heat and let stand for 2 minutes before serving.

Lunch & Dinner Entrées

SERVES 4
Prep Time: *10 minutes,*
plus marinating
Cooking Time: *14 minutes*

Honey Ginger Chicken with Noodles

¾ cup orange juice, divided
4 tablespoons teriyaki sauce, divided
4 tablespoons honey, divided
4 teaspoons crushed garlic, divided
1 teaspoon fresh grated ginger
1 pound boneless, skinless chicken breast, cut into strips
10 ounces dry spaghetti, broken in half
salt, to taste
1 head broccoli, cut in small pieces, or 1 pound snow peas
2 tablespoons sesame seeds (optional)

1. In a small bowl, combine ¼ cup orange juice, 2 tablespoons teriyaki, 2 tablespoons honey, 2 teaspoons garlic, and ginger. Add chicken strips; let marinate 20 minutes. In another small bowl, mix remaining orange juice, teriyaki, and honey and set aside.

2. Remove chicken from marinade, allowing excess to drip off. Place in Turbo Cooker base. Cover (valve closed) and cook on MEDIUM-HIGH heat 4 minutes.

3. Add the chicken marinade, stirring to coat strips. Cover (valve closed) and cook 2 minutes.

4. Remove cover and stir chicken. Transfer to a clean bowl and sprinkle with sesame seeds, if using.

5. Place pasta, 3 ¼ cups water, remaining garlic, and salt in base. Place steam rack in position. Place broccoli or snow peas and the bowl of chicken on rack. Cover (valve open) and cook 8 minutes. Turn off heat and stir in juice mixture. Let stand 2 minutes before serving.

Nutrition Facts Per Serving: 529 cal.; 38g protein; 3g fat; 80g carb.; 3g fiber; 66mg chol.

To reheat half the portion, place food along with ¼ cup orange juice in the Turbo Cooker. Cover (valve closed) and cook on MEDIUM heat 3 to 4 minutes. Stir twice during the reheating. Turn off heat; let stand 1 minute before serving.

Lunch & Dinner Entrées

*MAKES 4 BURGERS &
8 BROWNIES*
Prep Time: **10 minutes**
Cooking Time: **45 minutes**

Hungry, Hungry Burgers & Brownies

1 pound 98% lean ground beef
1 package dry onion soup mix
1 package (24 ounces) brownie mix
1 onion, sliced
8 ounces sliced mushrooms
2 teaspoons low-sodium beef bouillon concentrate
¼ teaspoon salt
½ cup candy covered chocolate, for garnish

1. In a bowl, blend the beef with the onion soup mix; form into 4 hamburgers and set aside.

2. Prepare brownie batter according to package directions. Pour brownie mixture into pan; place pan into steam rack. Pour 2 cups water into Turbo Cooker base. Place rack into position; cover (valve open), and cook on HIGH heat 15 minutes.

3. Pour additional 2 cups water into base. Place rack into position; cover (valve open) 15 minutes.

4. Remove lid and discard water from base. Place hamburgers and ⅓ cup water into base. Place rack into position; cover (valve closed) 3 minutes.

5. Flip hamburgers; add ¼ cup water. Place rack into position; cover (valve closed) 3 minutes.

6. Reduce heat to MEDIUM. Add 3 tablespoons water. With a spatula, gently move the hamburgers (so they don't stick). Place rack into position; cover (valve closed) 2 minutes.

7. Place hamburgers onto vegetable rack. Place steam rack onto vegetable rack and lock racks together. Place sliced onions and ¼ cup water into base. Place racks into position; cover (valve closed) 3 minutes.

8. Stir mushrooms, beef concentrate, salt and ⅓ cup water into base. Place racks into position; cover (valve closed) 4 minutes.

9. Sprinkle candy-coated chocolate on top of the brownies before serving.

Variation: For a richer flavor, substitute ⅓ cup half-and-half for the water in step 8.

Nutrition Facts Per Serving

Burgers: 241 cal.; 27g protein; 11g fat; 9g carb.; 2g fiber; 41mg chol.; 397mg sodium

Brownies: 223 cal.; 3g protein; 10g fat; 31g carb.; 1g fiber; 12mg chol.; 48mg sodium

Lunch & Dinner Entrées

SERVES 4
Prep Time: **5 minutes**
Cooking Time: **39 minutes**

Lamb Chops

½ teaspoon salt
¼ teaspoon pepper
1 teaspoon thyme
½ teaspoon granulated garlic
12 lamb chops, 3 ounces each
4 medium Idaho potatoes
3 cups fresh or frozen green beans

1. In a bowl, combine the salt, pepper, thyme, and granulated garlic. Rub the mixture onto the lamb chops.

2. Place potatoes and 4 cups water into base. Cover (valve closed) and cook on HIGH heat 30 minutes. Drain excess water, wrap potatoes in aluminum foil, and place onto steam rack.

3. Place lamb chops and ¼ cup water into base; place rack in position. Cover (valve closed) and cook on HIGH heat 3 minutes.

4. Turn lamb chops, add ¼ cup water. Place green beans on rack beside potatoes and place rack in position. Cover (valve closed) 4 minutes.

5. Reduce heat to MEDIUM. Turn lamb chops, add 1 tablespoon water, and place rack in position. Cover (valve closed) 2 minutes. Transfer lamb chops to serving plates and serve with beans and baked potato.

Nutrition Facts Per Serving: 479 cal.; 33g protein; 20g fat; 42g carb.; 5g fiber; 124mg chol.; 363mg sodium

To reheat half the portion, place food and ⅓ cup water into base. Cover (valve closed) and cook on MEDIUM heat 3 minutes. Add 2 table-spoons water. Cover (valve closed), 3 minutes. Turn off heat and let stand 1 minute before serving.

Manicotti with Cheese & Spinach

8 regular manicotti noodles
1 medium carrot, grated
1 medium onion, diced, divided
½ cup bread crumbs
2 tablespoons crushed fresh garlic, divided
½ cup chopped fresh basil, divided
1 teaspoon salt, divided
¾ teaspoon pepper, divided
2 cups fresh spinach, shredded
1½ cups light ricotta cheese
¼ cup low-fat grated Parmesan cheese
1 can (28 ounces) tomato sauce
2 teaspoons sugar
½ cup low-fat grated mozzarella cheese

1. Place noodles and 5 cups water into base; precook noodles on HIGH heat (valve open) 8 minutes. Drain noodles and let cool.

2. Place carrots, half the onion, bread crumbs, 1 tablespoon garlic, ¼ cup basil, ½ teaspoon salt, ¼ teaspoon pepper, and ⅓ cup water into base. Cover (valve closed) and cook on HIGH heat 3 minutes. Turn off heat. Stir in spinach, ricotta, and Parmesan.

3. Stuff manicotti with the cheese mixture and place onto steam rack. Set aside.

4. Place remaining onions and ⅓ cup water into base. Place rack into position. Cover (valve closed) and cook on HIGH heat 2 minutes.

To reheat half the portion, turn heat to HIGH and pour 1 cup water into the base. Place the leftover food into the steamer/poacher (use flat base) set on rack. Place rack into position, cover (valve closed) and cook 3 to 5 minutes. Open valve 1 to 2 minutes.

5. Reduce heat to MEDIUM-HIGH. Stir in tomato sauce, sugar, and remaining 1 tablespoon garlic. Place rack into position, cover (valve closed) 5 minutes.

6. Stir in remaining ½ teaspoon salt and ½ teaspoon pepper. Place rack into position. Cover (valve closed) 2 minutes.

7. Reduce heat to MEDIUM. Stir in remaining ¼ cup basil. Gently place manicotti into sauce and sprinkle with mozzarella cheese. Cover (valve closed) 3 minutes. Let sit 2 minutes before serving.

Variation: For a more exotic flavor, add 1 tablespoon fresh diced cilantro.

Nutrition Facts Per Serving: 366 cal.; 30g protein; 8g fat; 53g carb.; 6g fiber; 36mg chol.; 2039mg sodium

Sesame Beef

Lunch & Dinner Entrées

SERVES 4
Prep Time: **30 minutes**
Cooking Time: **14 minutes**

½ cup all-purpose flour
1 ½ teaspoons baking powder
¼ cup plus 2 teaspoons grilled sesame seeds
5 tablespoons cornstarch, divided
1 egg
¼ cup low-sodium soy sauce
¼ cup teriyaki sauce
½ cup brown sugar
2 tablespoons rice vinegar
2 teaspoons minced fresh garlic
⅓ cup canola oil
1 pound 98% lean beef, cut in strips
5 shallots, quartered

1. In a bowl, combine the flour, baking powder, ¼ cup sesame seeds, 2 tablespoons cornstarch, egg, and ¼ cup water. Let sit 15 minutes.

2. Meanwhile, in another bowl, combine the soy sauce, teriyaki, brown sugar, rice vinegar, garlic, remaining 3 tablespoons corn-starch, and ½ cup water.

3. Pour the oil into the base. Cover (valve closed) and cook on HIGH heat 3 minutes. (During this step, pass beef strips through flour mixture one by one.)

4. Place beef into base. Cover (valve closed) 2 minutes. Reduce heat to MEDIUM-HIGH. Gently turn beef. Cover (valve closed) 3 minutes.

5. Reduce heat to MEDIUM. Remove beef from base, set aside on a plate. Clean base with paper towel. Pour soy sauce mixture into base. Cover (valve closed) 2 minutes.

6. Stir sauce, add in beef and shallots. Cover (valve closed) 4 minutes.

7. Transfer to serving plate and top with remaining sesame seeds.

Variation: Add some sliced red peppers to this dish for garnish.

Nutrition Facts Per Serving: 200 cal.; 33g protein; 35g fat; 555g carb.; 13g fiber; 104mg chol.; 1476g sodium

To reheat half the portion, place the food and ⅓ cup water into base. Cover (valve closed) and cook on MEDIUM heat for 3 minutes. Add 2 tablespoons water, cover (valve closed) 3 minutes. Turn off heat; let stand 1 minute.

Stir-Fry Turkey with Cranberries

Lunch & Dinner Entrées

SERVES 4
Prep Time: **15 minutes**
Cooking Time: **14 minutes**

1 pound skinless, boneless turkey breast cutlets
2 tablespoons low-sodium soy sauce
1 tablespoon minced fresh ginger
1 teaspoon salt, divided
1 teaspoon granulated garlic
1 tablespoon low-sodium vegetable bouillon concentrate
1 ½ cups instant rice
1 sweet potato, peeled and cut into ⅛-inch-thick slices
1 ½ cups fresh cranberries
½ cup water chestnuts
¼ cup brown sugar
6 ounces whole berry cranberry sauce

1. In a bowl, marinate turkey in the soy sauce, minced ginger, ½ teaspoon salt, granulated garlic, and ½ cup water.

2. Into the Turbo Cooker base, place vegetable bouillon concentrate, remaining ½ teaspoon salt, and 2 cups water. Cover (valve closed) and cook on HIGH heat 4 minutes.

3. Place rice, with excess water, into a bowl. Place bowl onto steam rack. Remove turkey breast from marinade and reserve the marinade. Place turkey breast, sweet potato, and ¼ cup water into base. Place rack in position and cover (valve closed) 3 minutes.

4. Reduce heat to MEDIUM. Stir in fresh cranberries, the reserved marinade, and ⅓ cup water. Place rack in position. Cover (valve closed) 2 minutes.

To reheat half the portion, place the leftover turkey with rice and 2 tablespoons water into base. Cover (valve closed) and cook on MEDIUM-HIGH heat 2 minutes. Add 2 tablespoons water. Cover (valve closed) 2 minutes. Turn off heat and let stand 1 minute before serving.

5. Stir in water chestnuts, brown sugar, and cranberry sauce, and place rack in position. Cover (valve closed) 3 minutes.

6. Turn off heat and let sit 2 minutes.

Nutrition Facts Per Serving: 482 cal.; 32g protein; 23g fat; 82g carb.; 4g fiber; 68mg chol.; 1000g sodium

Veal Stuffed Shells

16 jumbo pasta shells
1½ pounds extra lean ground veal
½ cup bread crumbs
¾ teaspoon salt, divided
¼ teaspoon pepper
1 tablespoon crushed fresh garlic, divided
1 teaspoon dried basil, divided
½ teaspoon oregano
2 tablespoons fresh parsley
2 tablespoons grated low-fat Parmesan cheese
¼ cup white wine
½ onion, diced
1 tomato, diced
1 can (28 ounces) tomato sauce
½ teaspoon sugar
½ cup grated low-fat mozzarella cheese

1. Place shells in the Turbo Cooker with 3 cups water. Cover (valve closed) and cook on HIGH heat 9 minutes.

2. In a bowl, blend the veal with the breadcrumbs, ½ teaspoon salt, the pepper, ½ tablespoon crushed garlic, ½ teaspoon dried basil, oregano, parsley, grated Parmesan, and wine. When well blended, stuff meat mixture into shells and place onto steam rack.

3. Place onion and ⅓ cup water into base. Place rack into position, cover (valve closed) and cook on HIGH heat 2 minutes.

4. Stir in the diced tomatoes and remaining ½ tablespoon crushed garlic. Place rack into position, cover (valve closed) 3 minutes.

To preheat half the leftovers, place them into the base; turn heat to HIGH. Add ¼ cup water; cover (valve closed) and cook 3 minutes. Reduce heat to MEDIUM-HIGH. Gently move shells, cover (valve closed), 3 minutes. Turn off heat; let stand 2 minutes.

5. Reduce heat to MEDIUM. Stir in tomato sauce, sugar, remaining ¼ teaspoon salt, and ½ teaspoon dried basil. Place rack into position, cover (valve closed) 2 minutes.

6. Stir and gently place shells into sauce. Cover (valve closed) 3 minutes.

7. Reduce heat to MEDIUM-LOW. Sprinkle cheese on top of shells, cover (valve closed) 4 minutes. Turn off heat and let stand 1 minute. Garnish with parsley, if desired.

Nutrition Facts Per Serving: 588 cal.; 47g protein; 21g fat; 51g carb.; 5g fiber; 98mg chol.; 1922g sodium

Hoppy's Cheese Sticks

Snacks & Sandwiches

SERVES 4
Prep Time: **5 minutes**
Cooking Time: **12 minutes**

½ cup all-purpose flour
2 eggs
1 cup bread crumbs
¼ cup sesame seeds
¼ teaspoon salt
¼ teaspoon pepper
16 cheese sticks (2 ounces each), each cut in thirds
3 teaspoons vegetable oil, divided

1. Place flour into a bowl. In another bowl, beat the eggs. In a separate bowl, mix bread crumbs, sesame seeds, salt and pepper. Roll cheese pieces in flour mixture, then in eggs, then in bread crumbs.

2. Place ⅓ of the breaded cheese pieces, ½ teaspoon oil, and 2 tablespoons water into base. Cover (valve closed) and cook on MEDIUM-HIGH heat for 2 minutes.

3. Flip cheese sticks. Add ½ teaspoon oil and 1 tablespoon water. Cover (valve closed) for 2 minutes.

4. Place cooked cheese sticks onto rack. Repeat steps 2 and 3 (twice more) for remaining cheese pieces. Place rack into position and cover (valve closed) for 8 minutes.

5. Serve with mixed salad and whole wheat toast.

Nutrition Facts Per Serving: 464 cal.; 32g protein; 26g fat; 25g carb.; 1g fiber; 124mg chol.; 833mg sodium

Snacks & Sandwiches

SERVES 4
Prep Time: **15 minutes**
Cooking Time: **12 minutes**

Turbo Pan Pizza

1 package (¼ ounces) active dry yeast
1 tablespoon oil
1 cup all-purpose flour
1 teaspoon sugar
½ teaspoon salt
For the toppings
vegetables, such as green pepper, mushrooms, olives,
*   and onions, thinly sliced*
1 can (8 ounces) tomato sauce
½ teaspoon basil
½ teaspoon oregano
pepperoni slices
crumbled cooked sausage
1 cup grated low-fat mozzarella

1. In a medium bowl, combine the yeast with ½ cup hot water from the tap. Stir to mix. Add the oil, flour, sugar, and salt; stir until a ball of dough forms. Let stand 5 minutes.

2. Turn out dough onto a floured board. Knead until dough is stiff and then divide dough in half. Roll each half into a circle large enough to cover the Turbo Cooker base. Set aside.

3. Place vegetables in the base with 2 tablespoons water. Cover (valve closed) and cook on HIGH heat 3 minutes. Add the sauce, basil, and oregano. Stir; cover 1 minute.

4. Reduce heat to MEDIUM-HIGH. Clean out the base and add 1 round of dough. Cover (valve open) and cook 4 minutes.

5. Reduce heat to MEDIUM, flip dough with a spatula, and spread half sauce mixture over crust. Top with pepperoni and/or sausage, and half the cheese. Cover (valve closed); cook 4 minutes. Repeat with second crust.

Nutrition Facts Per Serving: 978 cal.; 49g protein; 53g fat; 77g carb.; 9g fiber; 79mg chol.

Prince Froggie's Royal Dessert

⅓ cup unsalted butter or margarine
10 ounces fat-free mini marshmallows
nonfat cooking spray
7 cups rice crisps cereal

1. Place butter in base, cover (valve closed) and cook on MEDIUM-HIGH heat for 1 minute.

2. Reduce heat to medium. Stir in marshmallows and cover (valve closed) 2 minutes.

3. Reduce heat to MEDIUM-LOW. Spray spatula with cooking spray and use it to stir cereal into mixture until well coated. Flatten mixture evenly against base; cover (valve closed) 3 minutes.

4. Turn off heat. Allow mixture to cool in pan. Invert onto a plate, cut into squares, and serve.

Nutrition Facts Per Serving: 545 cal.; 5g protein; 16g fat; 100g carb.; <1g fiber; 41mg chol.; 552g sodium

New York-Style Strawberry Cheesecake

1 ½ cups graham cracker crumbs
1 ¼ teaspoon salt, divided
1 ¾ cups sugar, divided
¼ cup ground almonds
¼ cup melted butter
nonfat cooking spray
5 medium eggs
3 packages (8 ounces each) low-fat cream cheese,
  cut in small pieces
¼ cup flour
2 ½ teaspoons lemon juice
½ teaspoon almond extract
1 teaspoon vanilla extract
1 cup sour cream
4 pints strawberries, rinsed and hulled

1. In a large bowl, combine the graham cracker crumbs, ¼ teaspoon salt, ¼ cup sugar, and the almonds. Mix in the melted butter.

2. Spray the springform pan with nonfat cooking spray. Pat the graham cracker mixture into the base of the pan and halfway up the sides.

3. Separate the eggs. Place whites in the freezer 5 minutes. Place yolks into another bowl. Using an electric mixer, beat in the cream cheese, 1 cup sugar, and remaining salt; beat until smooth. Sift flour into batter; add lemon juice, and almond and vanilla extracts. Blend until smooth. Add sour cream; blend well.

4. Clean the beaters. Remove egg whites from freezer and beat with ¼ cup sugar until stiff peaks form. Gently fold egg whites into batter. Blend well; pour batter into springform pan.

5. Replace the steamer/poacher insert with the springform pan. Add 2 ½ cups water. Cover (valve open); cook on HIGH heat 10 minutes.

6. Reduce heat to MEDIUM-HIGH. Add 1 cup water; cover (valve closed) 10 minutes. Increase heat to HIGH. Add 2 ½ cups water; cover (valve open) and cook 10 minutes. Reduce heat to MEDIUM-HIGH. Add 1 ¼ cups water; cover (valve closed) 10 minutes. Increase heat to HIGH. Add 2 cups water; cover (valve open) 10 minutes.

7. Add 2 cups water. Cover (valve closed) 10 minutes. Turn off heat, open valve, and let sit 20 minutes. Remove springform pan. Let stand 1 hour and then refrigerate.

8. To serve, top cake with 1 pint of the strawberries. Mix remaining strawberries in blender with ¼ cup sugar. Blend until smooth and glaze cake with mixture.

Nutrition Facts Per Serving: 440 cal.; 13g protein; 21g fat; 53g carb.; 2g fiber; 133mg chol.

Vita-Mix

Vita-Mix has the distinction of being the oldest company in The *As Seen on TV Cookbook*. Founded in the early 1920s by self-taught salesman W. G. Barnard, Vita-Mix has been in the business of selling "modern" home products for a long time—and it has almost always been a step ahead of the competition.

Case in point: When television debuted in 1949, it wasn't long before Vita-Mix booked a 30-minute spot and broadcast the world's first infomercial.

The early Vita-Mix blenders did pretty much what you'd expect: Blend, purée, liquefy. But according to Vita-Mix, the newest models, including the Super 5000, can do the work of "10 different kitchen appliances." With a 2-horsepower motor—the size of a small boat motor—it's certainly powerful enough to blend just about anything you can put in it.

This little powerhouse can blend smoothies in 60 seconds, whip cream, crush a half-gallon of ice in three seconds, purée fresh baby food, and grind grains for flour.

The most surprising feature of the Vita-Mix is that it can blend and *cook* soup: The cutting blades of the Super 5000 rotate at 240 miles per hour, generating enough friction heat to cook a half-gallon of soup to steaming hot. Now *that's* ingenious.

MAKES 4 CUPS
Prep Time: **4 minutes**
Cooking Time: **None**

Bacon Cheddar Potato Soup

2 cups skim milk
2 medium Yukon gold potatoes, divided
⅓ cup cheddar cheese
¼ small onion, sautéed
½ teaspoon dill weed
½ teaspoon rosemary
½ teaspoon salt
3 slices bacon, crispy, and crumbled

1. Place milk, 1 potato, cheese, onion, dill, rosemary, and salt in Vita-Mix container.

2. Secure 2-part lid. Select VARIABLE, speed #1. Turn on machine and quickly increase speed to #10, then to HIGH. Run for 4 minutes or until heavy steam flows through lid opening.

3. Add salt. Reduce speed to VARIABLE, speed, #3. Remove lid plug. Drop in reserved potato and bacon. Run just until chopped and then stop machine. Serve immediately.

Nutrition Facts Per Serving: 161 cal.; 10g protein; 6g fat; 20g carb.; 1g fiber; 16mg chol.; 493g sodium

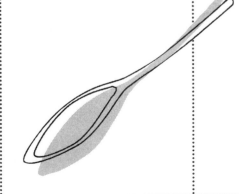

Chicken Potato Spinach Soup

Lunch & Dinner Entrées

SERVES 4
Prep Time: **3 to 4 minutes**
Cooking Time: **5 minutes**

1 small onion
1 teaspoon lite margarine
3 medium potatoes, baked or boiled, with or
    without skin, divided
3 chicken bouillon cubes
⅛ teaspoon rosemary
2 cups skim milk, steaming
½ cup lite liquid nondairy creamer or half-and-half
1 tablespoon cooked or frozen spinach
1 chicken breast, skinned, boned, cooked, and cut up

1. In a medium skillet, saute onion in margarine until translucent.

2. Place the onion, 2 potatoes, bouillon, rosemary, and hot skim milk in Vita-Mix container.

3. Secure 2-part lid. Select VARIABLE, speed #1. Turn on machine and quickly increase speed to #10, then to HIGH. Run for 2 to 3 minutes or until steaming hot.

4. Reduce speed to VARIABLE, speed #3. Remove the lid plug, add the creamer, and then drop in the spinach and the chicken. Run until chicken is chopped, about 15 seconds. Drop in reserved potato and run for an additional 5 seconds. Serve immediately.

Variation: Use vegetable bouillon cubes, and omit chicken and chicken bouillon to make this recipe suitable for vegetarian diets.

Nutrition Facts Per Serving: 179 cal.; 14g protein; 1g fat; 31g carb.; 2g fiber; 20mg chol.; 373g sodium

Side Dishes

SERVES 6
Prep Time: **7 minutes**
Cooking Time: **None**

Reuben Soup

2 small to medium potatoes (Yukon Gold or red skin)
2 cups milk
¼ teaspoon white pepper
½ teaspoon garlic salt
½ teaspoon celery salt
½ teaspoon lemon pepper seasoning
¼ teaspoon salt
½ cup to 1 cup Swiss cheese, cut in large chunks
½ teaspoon caraway seeds
1 tablespoon Thousand Island dressing
1 tablespoon sweet pickle relish
½ cup sauerkraut
½ cup to 1 cup corned beef
rye croutons, for garnish

1. Place the potatoes, milk, white pepper, garlic salt, celery salt, lemon pepper, and salt in Vita-Mix container.

2. Secure 2-part lid. Select VARIABLE, speed #1. Turn on machine and quickly increase speed to #10, then to HIGH. Run for 4 minutes or until heavy steam escapes through the lid plug opening.

3. Reduce speed to VARIABLE, speed #5. Remove lid plug and drop in cheese. Run for 1 minute. Add caraway seeds, dressing, relish, sauerkraut and corned beef. Run for an additional 10 seconds, or until beef is just chopped. If necessary, use the tamper to press any ingredients into the blades while processing. Serve immediately, garnished with croutons.

Nutrition Facts Per Serving: 303 cal.; 17g protein; 8g fat; 41g carb.; 5g fiber; 42mg chol.; 881g sodium

Tofu Alfredo Pasta Sauce

Lunch & Dinner Entrées

MAKES 1 ½ CUPS
Prep Time: **3 to 4 minutes**
Cooking Time: **None**

¾ cup soft tofu
¾ cup fat-free cottage cheese
2 tablespoons fat-free cream cheese
¼ teaspoon garlic salt
3 tablespoons Parmesan cheese
2 tablespoons Romano cheese
2 tablespoons butter or lite margarine
¼ teaspoon white pepper

1. Place the tofu, cottage cheese, cream cheese, garlic salt, Parmesan and Romano cheeses, butter, and white pepper in Vita-Mix container.

2. Secure 2-part lid. Select VARIABLE, speed #1. Turn on machine and quickly increase speed to #10, then to HIGH. Run for 3 to 4 minutes.

3. Serve over steamed vegetables or pasta.

Note: If sauce is too thick, thin with milk to desired consistency.

Nutrition Facts Per 1½ cups: 586 cal.; 47g protein; 38g fat; 15g carb.; <1g fiber; 88mg chol.; 1885g sodium

California Salsa

¼ cup fresh cilantro
½ medium onion
1 teaspoon fresh lemon juice
6 ripe roma tomatoes, quartered
1 Serrano chili pepper
1 teaspoon cider vinegar
1 teaspoon salt (optional)

1. Place the cilantro, onion, lemon juice, tomatoes, pepper, vinegar, and salt in Vita-Mix container.

2. Secure 2-part lid. Select VARIABLE, speed #1. Turn on machine and quickly increase speed to #4 or #5. Run for 5 to 10 seconds or until ingredients are chopped to desired consistency. If necessary, use the tamper to push the ingredients into the blades while processing. Do not overmix. Serve with tortilla chips.

Nutrition Facts Per 2 ½ cups: 120 cal.; 5g protein; 1g fat; 27g carb.; 6g fiber; <1mg chol.; 40g sodium

Hummus

1 can (15 ounces) chickpeas (garbanzos), drained
½ cup raw sesame seeds
1 tablespoon olive oil
¼ cup lemon juice
1 clove garlic
salt, to taste

Snacks & Sandwiches

MAKES 1½ CUPS
Prep Time: **1 minute**
Cooking Time: **1 minute**

1. Place the chickpeas, sesame seeds, olive oil, lemon juice, garlic, and salt in Vita-Mix container.

2. Secure 2-part lid. Select VARIABLE, speed #1. Turn on machine and quickly increase speed to #10, then to HIGH. Run machine for 1 minute or until smooth. If necessary, use the tamper to push the ingredients into the blades while processing.

Nutrition Facts Per 1½ cups: 1057 cal.; 34g protein; 54g fat; 119g carb.; 28g fiber; <1mg chol.; 1281g sodium

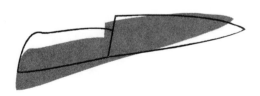

Snacks & Sandwiches

MAKES 1 ¼ CUPS
Prep Time: **1 minute**
(see Caution)
Cooking Time: **None**

Peanut or Cashew Butter

24 ounces roasted peanuts or cashews

1. Pour nuts into Vita-Mix container.

2. Secure 2-part lid. Select VARIABLE, speed #1. Insert tamper through lid opening. Turn on machine and quickly increase speed to #10, then to HIGH. Use the tamper to push the nuts into the blades. In 1 minute you will hear a high-pitched chugging sound. Once the butter begins to flow freely through the blades the motor sound will change from a high pitch to a low laboring sound. Stop and pour into container.

3. Refrigerate in airtight container.

Variation: For Almond Butter, substitute roasted almonds. Add ½ cup oil if necessary. Refrigerate and pour off excess oil next day.

Caution: Overprocessing will cause serious overheating to your machine! Do not process for more than 1 minute after mixture starts circulating freely.

Nutrition Facts Per 1-ounce Serving: 166 cal.; 7g protein; 14g fat; 6g carb.; 2g fiber; <1mg chol.; 1g sodium

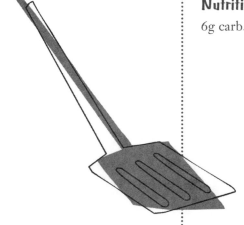

Mixed Fruit Smoothie

½ cup frozen strawberries, sweetened
1 banana
½ orange, including white part of peel
¼ cup frozen peaches
½ cup plain nonfat yogurt
¼ cup ice cubes

1. Place the strawberries, banana, orange, peaches, yogurt, and ice cubes in Vita-Mix container.

2. Secure 2-part lid. Select VARIABLE, speed #1. Turn on machine and quickly increase speed to #10, then to HIGH. Run for 1 minute or until smooth. Serve immediately.

Nutrition Facts Per Serving: 134 cal.; 3g protein; <1g fat; 34g carb.; 4g fiber; 1mg chol.; 21g sodium

Beverages

SERVES 2
Prep Time: **1 minute**
Cooking Time: **None**

Orange Juice Plus

2 medium navel oranges, peeled and quartered
¾ cup ice cubes
¼ teaspoon vanilla extract (optional)
1 tablespoon sugar or other sweetener, to taste (optional)

1. Place the oranges, ¼ cup water, ice cubes, vanilla, and sugar, if using, in Vita-Mix container.

2. Secure 2-part lid. Select VARIABLE, speed #1. Turn on machine and quickly increase speed to #10, then to HIGH. Run for 1 minute or until smooth. Serve immediately.

Variation: Add ½ cup pineapple with juice.

Note: For plain orange juice, omit vanilla and sweetener.

Nutrition Facts Per Serving: 90 cal.; 1g protein; <1g fat; 23g carb.; 3g fiber; 0mg chol.; 2g sodium

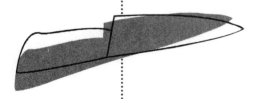

Strawberry Yogurt Freeze

Beverages

SERVES 2
Prep Time: **30 to 60
seconds**
Cooking Time: **None**

1 cup plain, vanilla, or strawberry nonfat yogurt
3 cups frozen strawberries, sweetened (If using whole frozen
*   strawberries, add ⅓ cup sugar or other sweetener, to taste)*

1. Place the yogurt and strawberries in Vita-Mix container.

2. Secure 2-part lid. Select VARIABLE, speed #1. Turn on
machine and quickly increase speed to #10, then to HIGH. Use
tamper to press ingredients into the blades while processing. In
30 to 60 seconds, the sound of the motor will change and four
mounds should form in the mixture. Stop machine. Do not
overmix or mixture will melt. Serve immediately.

Variation: Use other frozen fruit and yogurt flavors, such as
blueberries or peaches.

Nutrition Facts Per Serving: 319cal.; 7g protein; 0g fat; 75g carb.;
5g fiber; 0mg chol.; 89g sodium

The Original Toblerone® Fondue

For the Fondue

1 cup heavy cream, heated to simmer

14 ounces Toblerone bars, finely chopped

2 tablespoons cognac or hazelnut-flavored coffee syrup

For the Dippers

bananas

fresh or canned pineapple chunks

marshmallows

pound cake

sliced apples

sliced pears

sponge cake

strawberries

1. Place the warmed cream, Toblerone, and cognac in Vita-Mix container in order listed.

2. Secure 2-part lid. Select VARIABLE, speed #1. Turn on machine and quickly increase speed to #4. Run for 30 seconds. Pour mixture into fondue pot; serve with dippers.

Nutrition Facts Per Serving: 378 cal.; 3g protein; 26g fat; 32g carb.; 0g fiber; 41mg chol.; 12g sodium

Order Now!
How to Purchase
Your Favorite Kitchen
Gadgets

Donut Express

800-610-7758

www.emsontv.com

**George Foreman Lean Mean Contact Roasting Machine
& Lean Mean Fat Reducing Grilling Machine**

888-889-0899

www.esalton.com

Jack LaLanne Power Juicer

800-229-2178

www.jacksjuicer.com

Pasta Pro

800-972-1616

www.pastapro.com

Perfect Pancake

1-800-361-9449
www.perfectpancake.com

Ronco Showtime Rotisserie & Barbecue Oven

800-486-1806
http://shop.ronco.com

Turbo Cooker

888-591-9850
www.chefrandall.com

Vita-Mix

800-848-2649
www.vitamix.com